A History Of
Leadville Theater

A History of Leadville Theater

Opera Houses, Variety Acts and Burlesque Shows

Gretchen Scanlon

The History Press

Published by The History Press
Charleston, SC 29403
www.historypress.net

Cover images: Leadville theater group. *Courtesy of the Colorado Mountain History Collection, available at the Lake County Public Library*.

First published 2012

Manufactured in the United States

ISBN 978.1.60949.711.8

Library of Congress CIP data applied for.

I dedicate this book to my mother, Maureen Scanlon, who has always been my biggest supporter.

In memory of
Evelyn Furman, her dedication, not only to the Tabor Opera House, to save this amazing building, but also in telling the story. Evelyn inspired me to tell the story of all these theaters.

Contents

Acknowledgements

Thank you to Janice Fox, Lake County Public Library, for all the hours helping me find just the right photo and for all the time we spent trading stories about Leadville's amazing history.

Thank you to all of my friends and family members, for all the hours listening to my stories of theaters, actors and plays. Your excitement and encouragement let me know that these were stories worth telling.

Introduction

Theaters were found in Williamsburg, Virginia; New York City; and Charleston, South Carolina, in the early 1700s. After the Revolutionary War, the government relaxed its laws regarding theaters, causing a mass expansion, and by the early 1800s, there was one in most sizable towns in the East.

Variety theaters, commonly referred to as "wine or illegitimate theaters," were the first type offered. Usually, they did not charge admission—attendees were expected to visit the bar. They offered a diverse selection of performances: singing, comedy sketches, gymnastics, boxing, tightrope walking and trapeze acts. It was as though you were watching a circus on a small scale, with monkeys and dogs as part of the show. The theaters employed a band or orchestra to accompany the acts, and the musicians stayed with the theaters while the troupes moved on to the next town after a few months.

The legitimate theaters offered classic plays by famous authors such as Shakespeare, typically run by a stock company, and put on a different play every few days. This presented a challenge for those learning lines for a new show during the day and performing a different show at night. Companies usually had a leading lady and man, popular in that particular town but not well known elsewhere. Many actors got their start with a stock company; as their fame grew, they left the company and signed on with traveling shows. Many child actors were discovered when they were put on the stage by a parent who was in the cast.

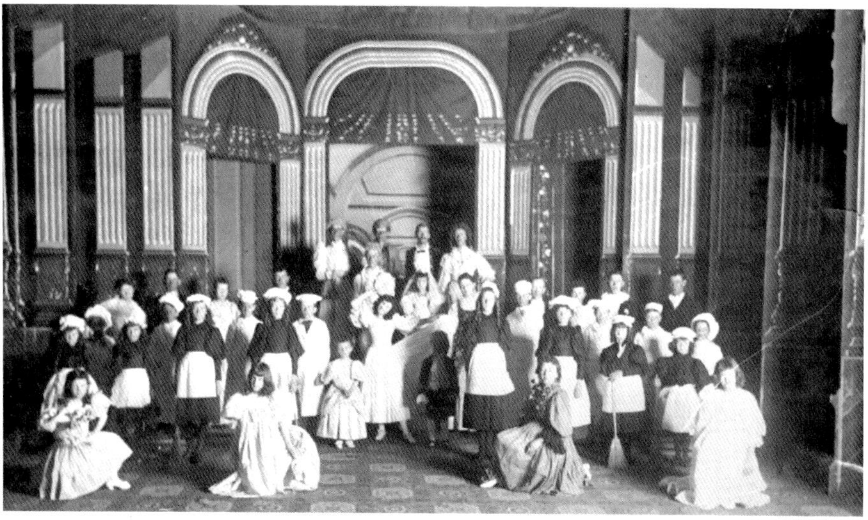

The Leadville theater group in about 1880. *Courtesy of the Colorado Mountain History Collection, Lake County Public Library.*

With the expansion of the railroad, stock companies were pushed into smaller, less popular theaters and were almost eliminated by the 1900s. In order to survive, they took their show on the road, where they played at one theater for a few weeks, performing five or six different plays. They did not travel as far as the larger companies but rather stayed in small regions.

Companies traveled west before the railroad, but the trip was costly, and few were willing to foot the bill for such a venture. They traveled by wagon, bringing all the necessary scenery and props. Other actors would travel by themselves, booking a theater for a few weeks as a guest with the stock company and then moving on.

The earliest theaters in Lake County were in Oro City and Sacramento City, but little is known of those early playhouses. Jack Langrishe and J.M. Dougherty were actors who joined forces in 1861 to bring the theater to small mining camps in Colorado. Langrishe's troupe arrived in Oro City and rented a small log cabin, calling it the "People's Theater." J.M. Dougherty, Jack Langrishe and Jack's wife, Jeanette, were the principal actors and brought plays such as *Othello*, *Uncle Tom's Cabin* and *Hamlet* to the booming mining town.

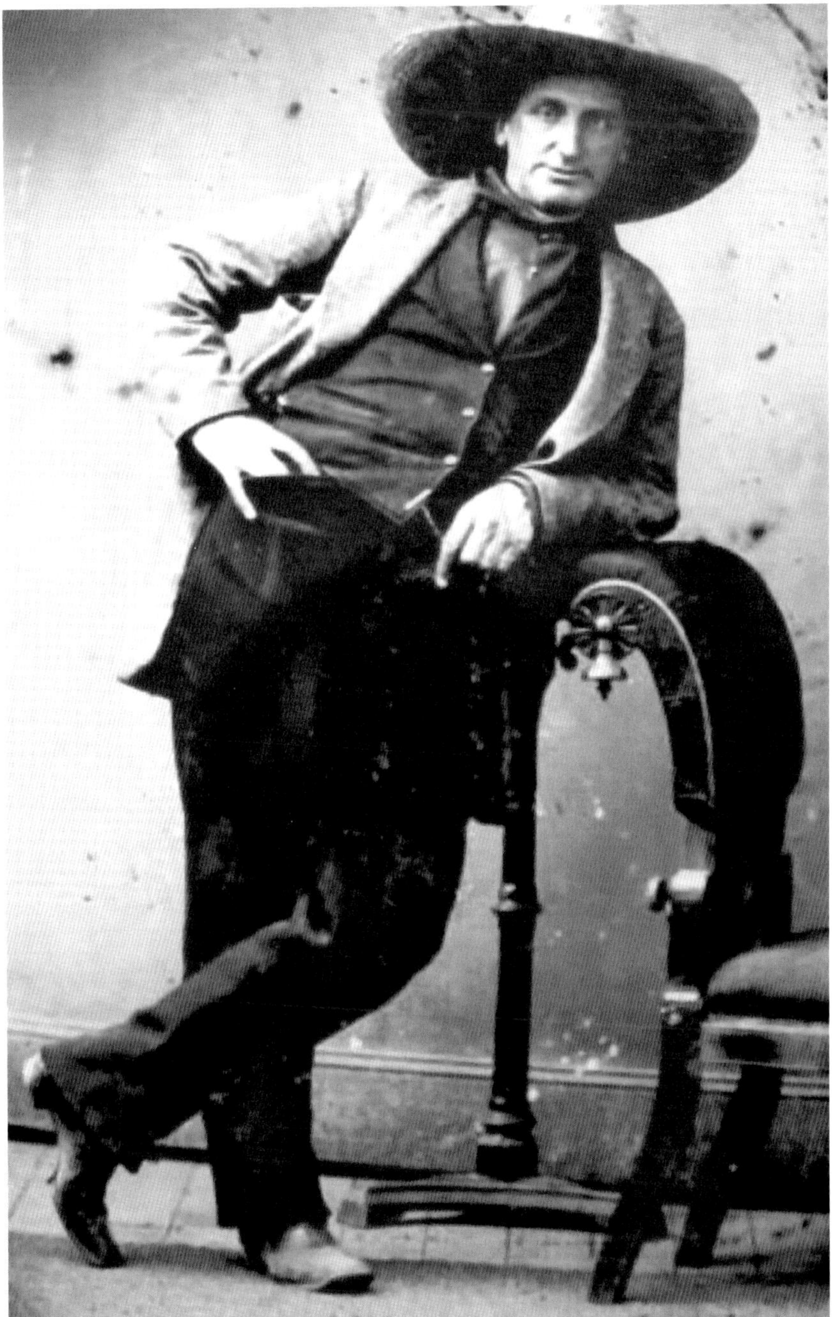

Jack Langrishe.

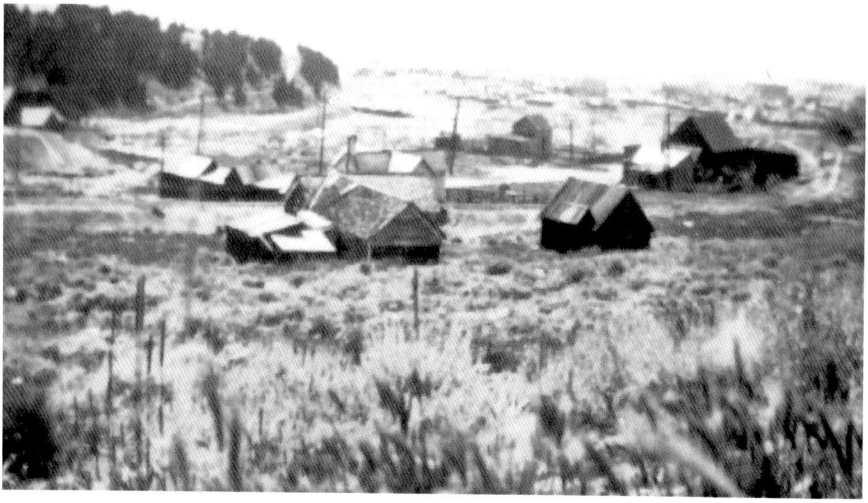

Oro City. *Courtesy of the Colorado Mountain History Collection, Lake County Public Library.*

An article in the *Rocky Mountain News* reported that Oro City had three theaters in 1862. Troupes continued coming to Oro City over the next several years, setting up a stage in a tent or in the back of a bar for the summer, leaving town during the harsh winter and returning the following spring.

THEATERS OF THE CARBONATE CAMP

Leadville, the county seat of Lake County, Colorado, sits at 10,152 feet above sea level and is the highest incorporated city in the United States. In the 1880s, it was one of the richest silver camps in the nation and the second-largest city in the state, with more than thirty thousand people. Established in 1878, it had several nicknames: "Carbonate Camp," "Two Mile-High City," "Cloud City" and "Magic City."

State Street was known as the wickedest street in the nation, with bordellos, cribs, saloons, dance halls and variety theaters. Brass bands paraded up and down the street drumming up patrons. Chestnut Street, the original main thoroughfare, housed the majority of businesses; due to many fires, most of the buildings are gone. Harrison Avenue was the location of the more legitimate businesses and is now the main street.

One of the first people to offer entertainment in the Carbonate Camp was William Nye. He opened a saloon early in 1877, a small frame building twenty-four by sixty feet. He was well known in California Gulch, opening saloons in Oro City in the early '60s, returning in '74 and the following year in Malta. Nye saw the potential of Malta, purchased all the un-owned lots, improved the roads and built a saloon and a city pavilion—a place to hold dances.

One of the most famous lecturers at Nye's Saloon was Susan B. Anthony, who visited in the fall of 1877. Before her lecture, Nye purchased yards of calico fabric to cover the liquor supplies behind the bar. The saloon was packed to capacity, and people lined the street to hear the

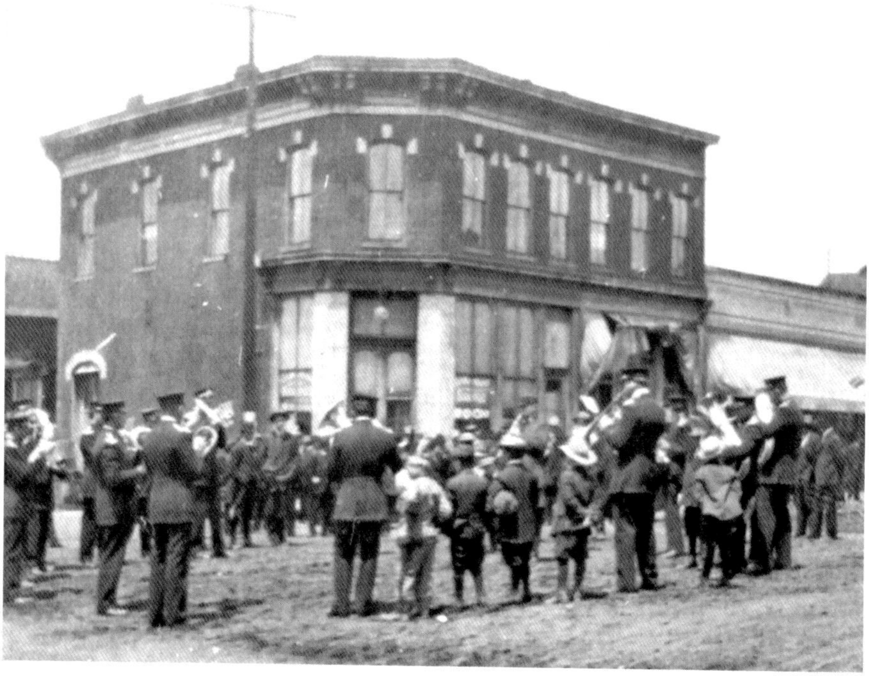

A brass band playing in Leadville in about 1885. *Courtesy of the Colorado Mountain History Collection, Lake County Public Library.*

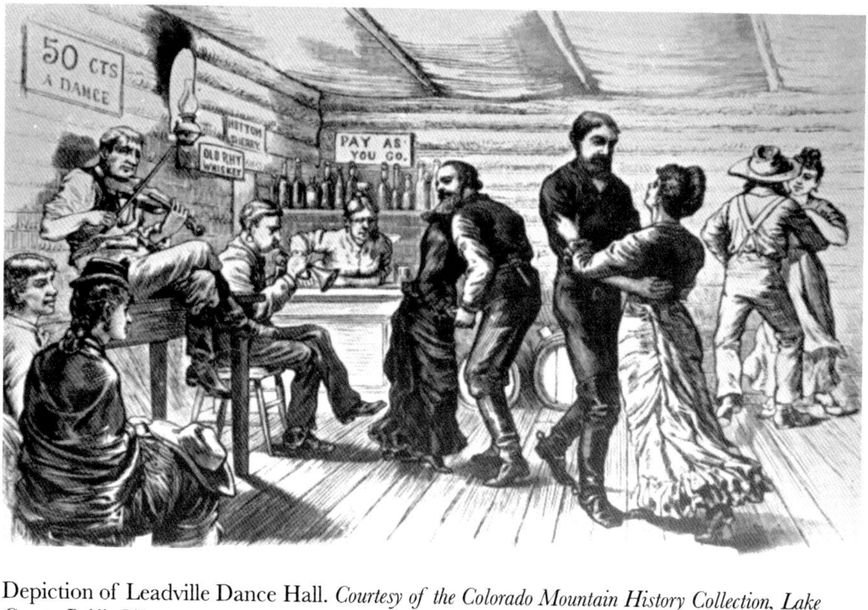

Depiction of Leadville Dance Hall. *Courtesy of the Colorado Mountain History Collection, Lake County Public Library.*

famous suffragist. Governor John Routt and his wife were in town for Mrs. Anthony's lecture—he even stood by her side as she spoke. Other then Routt's wife, Eliza, only a few women attended.

Susan B. Anthony was in Colorado to speak to voters about the ballot issue that would allow women the right to vote. She said that the crowd that night was the roughest group she had ever encountered—although when the men noticed that the smoke was making her cough, they happily snuffed out their pipes. Mrs. Anthony asked for donations; a hat was passed around the room and soon overflowed with gold dust and nuggets.

Although the miners seemed to enjoy her elegant speech, the vote was defeated in October. Sixteen years later, Colorado was the first state to adopt an amendment giving women the right to vote.

In 1879, the newly formed City of Leadville enacted a business fee. Certain businesses were required to pay a licensing fee, including saloons, ball alleys (early bowling alleys), billiard rooms, hacks, peddlers, lumberyards, brewers, theaters and so on. Theaters were broken into two groups, variety or legitimate. The price for a variety theater was $150 per quarter, and a legitimate theater was $10 per performance or $50 per quarter. In addition, most served alcohol and had to have a liquor license, which cost $500 per year.

The *Carbonate Chronicle* ran an article on wages in February, 1880, reporting that good waitresses made $15 to $25 per week; variety-actor couples made $100 to $175 per week, and good leading singles ranged from $50 to $125 per week. The lowest-paid actors made $15 to $35 per week.

The Coliseum Novelty Theater

The Coliseum Novelty Theater was the first theater to open in the Carbonate Camp, in 1877. It was a small wood-frame building at 134 West Chestnut Street and had sleeping rooms upstairs that rented for a nightly rate. Many ladies employed as waitresses and dance hall girls at the house rented these rooms. Entering the building, you passed through the gaming rooms on your way to the theater in the back. Tiered box seats lined the walls on either side of this magnificent theater. Anyone who bought a drink could enter, but there was an extra charge for a box seat.

When the Coliseum opened, it was a variety theater, with dancing girls, dogfights, cockfights, wrestling and boxing matches. It had a promotional wagon, covered in advertising posters and the band loaded in the back, while high-stepping horses pulled it though the streets.

On June 15, 1879, there was a fire at the Coliseum set by an arsonist. Two other adjoining buildings were also destroyed; one was the Miners' Arms Saloon. "Curly" Mack, a fireman, contracted pneumonia from exposure and died a few days later.

J.B. Overman, half-owner of Overman and McCarthy Produce on Chestnut Street, was looking for an investment, and in the winter of 1880, he leased the Coliseum. It was in need of repair, so he shut it down for renovations.

On April 16, 1880, two days after it was reopened, shots were heard coming from the theater, and a rush of men exited the building, hoping not to get hit with a flying bullet. J.B. Overman shot and killed Thomas

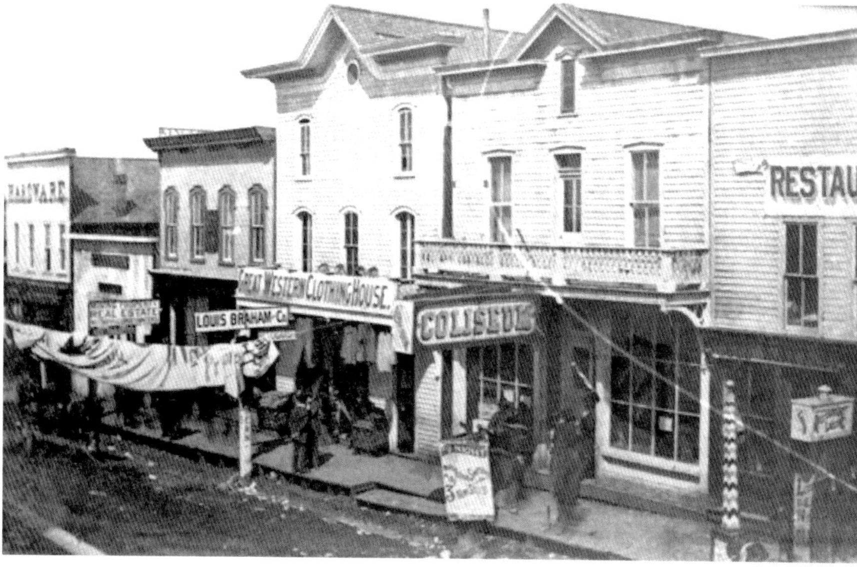

The Coliseum Theater in about 1878. *Courtesy of the Colorado Mountain History Collection, Lake County Public Library.*

Nugent. He told police that "earlier in the evening, Mr. Nugent and his friends were drinking in one of the boxes. They got into an altercation with a waitress and Nugent slapped the waitress, pushing her out of the box." She was unhurt, but this made Overman angry; he saw the men at the bar and confronted them, telling them to leave his theater. Nugent refused, making some remark that he would leave when he wanted. Overman replied, "This is my house and I am running it." Laughing, Nugent pointed to his friends and replied, "Me and my gang plan to run it from here on," then backed Overman into a corner and told him, "I will fix you." When he thought that Nugent started reaching for a gun, Overman fired several shots, hitting Nugent in the chest. Falling to the floor, Nugent said to his men, "I am gone, boys." The shooting was found to be in self-defense, but Overman was done with the theater business, leasing it to Con Caddigan and Charlie Search.

While Caddigan was the manager, evenings ended with a performance called "Female Bathers," an act described as "naughty but nice" that was designed to get men in the door. Once they had a drink in hand, it was easy to keep them there for more imbibing. Caddigan ran the theater along with the Grand Central Theater for a few months, but then his duties at Grand Central began to take too much of his time.

Jeff Winney's California Free Concert Hall

Caddigan leased the theater to Jeff Winney in November 1880, renaming it Jeff Winney's California Free Concert Hall; it quickly became known as one of Leadville's notorious dives. Newspapers were littered with tales of young men looking for the wilder side. They wandered into the hall and were offered drinks until they passed out. The next day, they usually woke up in an alley with their possessions gone.

One of Winney's advertisements for hiring read, "Waiter Girls Wanted; must appear in short clothes or no engagement." Once, Winney was arrested for using women to serve beer and entice men into his house of sin. He demanded a jury trial, and after the evidence was heard, the jury came back with a not guilty verdict. Possibly one or more of the men on jury had patronized Winney's place.

One night, one of the most popular ladies at Winney's was seated at a table in the gaming rooms. Kitty Crawhurst, a dark-eyed, dark-haired beauty, whose hair reached the hem of her dress, was Leadville's well-known lady gambler. She played a game called "Rolling Faro." Asked why she chose to become a gambler, she explained, "My husband owned a restaurant in Chicago, and heard of the fortunes being made in Leadville; he sold the restaurant and came here to make his own fortune. Soon after he arrived, he took ill, and the cost of the nurse used all the money. Fearing I would never see him again, I came to Leadville, but could not find a job to pay the bills. My husband began to gamble but his luck was not good; I joined him at the tables, and found I was a very good gambler."

Gambling limits in most towns ranged from about $20 to $50. Bat Masterson came here in 1880, where single hands could go from $1 to $1,000. He wandered into Winney's to play with Kitty Crawhurst; her reputation preceded her. He played a few nights with Kitty and then left Leadville. He told friends that he planned to reinvest his winnings in Leadville; however, property values were too high.

The theater/dance hall ended its short history at 12:15 a.m. on June 21, 1881, when it caught fire and burned to the ground. The female employees

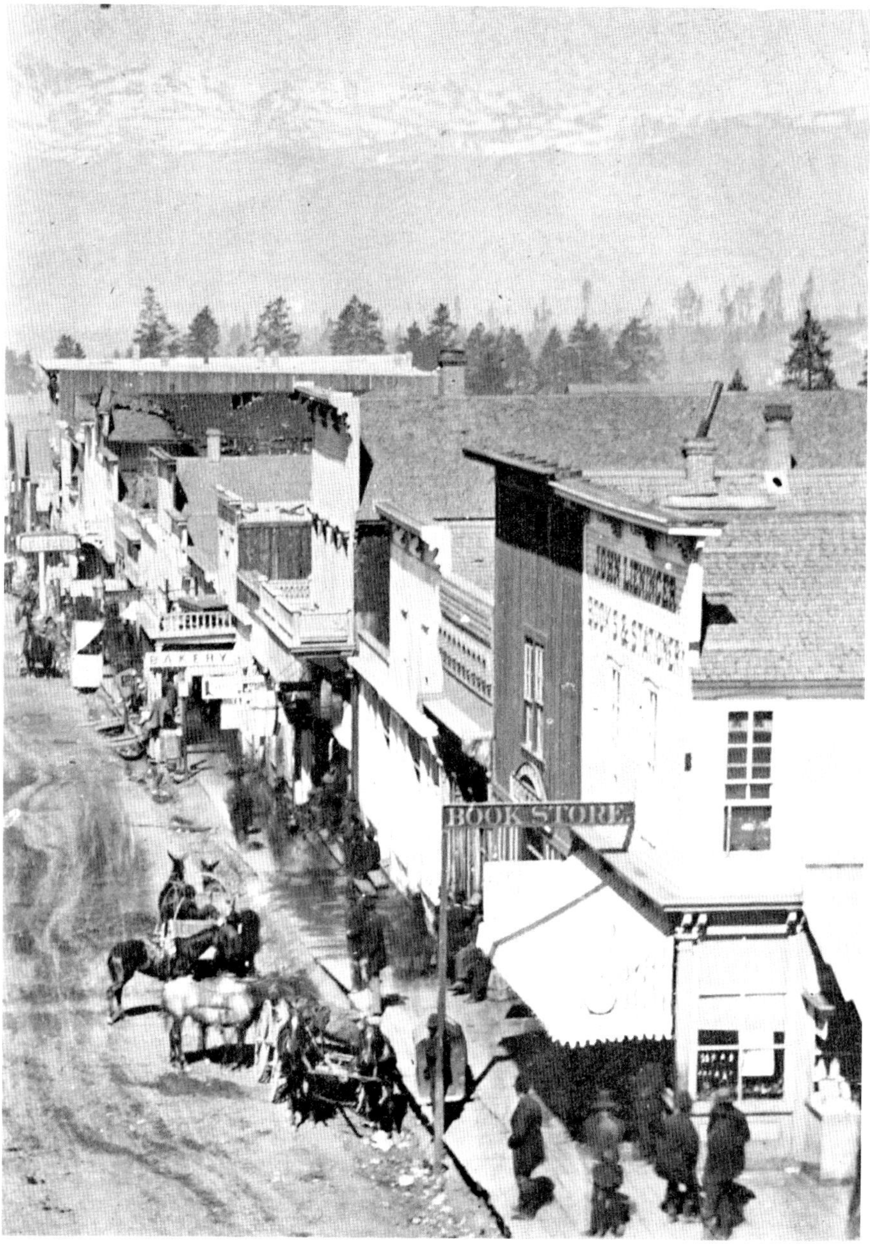

The Coliseum Theater after a 1879 fire. *Courtesy of the Colorado Mountain History Collection, Lake County Public Library.*

rushed out, in the barest attire; all their costumes were lost in the blaze. Con Caddigan along with George Wright and C.N. Fish—two firemen from Humphreys Hose Company—were fighting the blaze on the roof when the second story gave way. The men became trapped in the interior, and a cry was heard from the crowd, "My god, they will burn to death!"

At this, the crowd rushed forward to rescue them, but the police pushed them back. Caddigan managed to climb out of the blazing inferno, suffering minor burns. When the firemen saw Caddigan come out alive, it spurred them on to find their comrades. After an hour of being buried, Wright was the first to be found, though he was badly burned. Next, they followed the sounds of groans to Mr. Fish. It took another hour to free him, but his injuries were less severe. Bouben Ponnanski, another fireman, was on a ladder when he fell thirty feet, sustaining a large gash to his temple. All four men survived and returned to work after a few weeks.

The only man to be killed that day was Victor LeBrun. He was walking down Chestnut Street and must not have heard the alarm bells. He stepped in front of the hose wagon charging down the street and was struck by the wagon tongue. He survived for several days before the doctor discovered a large bolt embedded in his lower back. The bolt was removed, but he died a few days later. After the fire, Jeff Winney purchased another saloon and continued to operate it for a few years.

At the time, the cause of the fire was not known, but some suspected an arsonist. It was not until August that the cause was revealed—the arsonist lit several more fires, including one at the Academy of Music.

The Comique Theater

Early in 1878, Frank Stanselle purchased 109–111 State Street. It had been a bowling alley, and Stanselle did some minor remodeling before reopening it as a theater. He quickly sold it to Thomas Kemp, who had recently moved from Pueblo, where he had owned the Theatre Comique, a favorite hangout of Bat Masterson and Doc Holiday. Kemp finished remodeling and opened on June 12, turning his building into one of Leadville's earliest and most popular theaters.

It was a one-and-a-half-story, wood-frame building, fifty by one hundred feet. A saloon and the gambling rooms were in the front. A ticket taker stood at the door, taking money, and the theater was in the rear. The prop rooms were in the basement, and dressing rooms were under the stage.

As you entered the theater, you saw the large proscenium arch, said to be a little more than a bunch of unpainted boards, along with oil lamps lining the stage as footlights. The stage was fitted with a large red velvet curtain embossed with gold letters "T.C." and a crudely painted advertisement. Oil lamps, hanging from the rafters, provided some low light. It was a drafty building, heated with two coal-burning stoves.

There were private boxes on the sides and back of the theater, with tables down front and the stage in the back. The boxes were built against the walls, with little elevation. Seeing the stage was almost impossible—these boxes were built more for privacy than to see the show. The first orchestra employed by the theater was a piano player and two violinists, who were seated to the side of the stage.

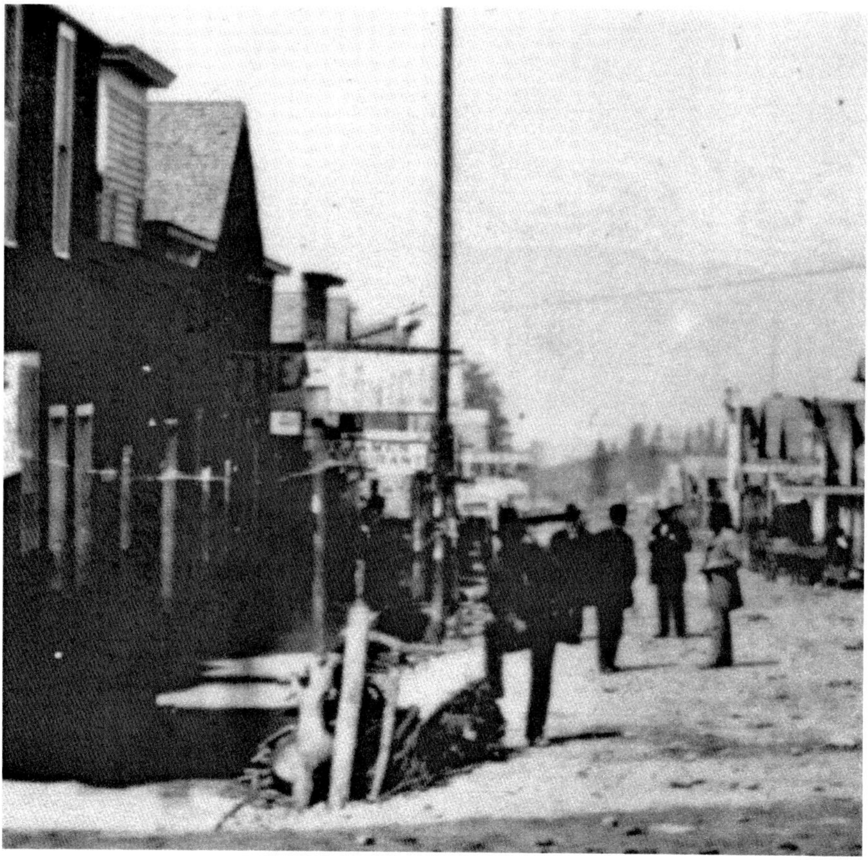

The Comique Theater on State Street in about 1878. *Courtesy of the Colorado Mountain History Collection, Lake County Public Library.*

The Comique could seat five hundred people on the floor and in the saloon and card rooms. There was seating for another four hundred people in the boxes, bringing the total to nine hundred. Admission was only charged for special performances, like ladies' night, when the bars and game rooms were closed.

In the back of the theater was a rough wooden bar, painted brown, with lines of gleaming glasses ready to serve. The Comique employed several waitresses to serve drinks; they were young and pretty, and their dresses were thought of as lurid. As soon as the curtain went down, the girls were instructed to become acquainted with the gentlemen in the boxes.

Charles Dow, who founded the *Wall Street Journal* and cofounded the Dow Jones Company, wrote about his visits to the Comique in one of the *Leadville Letters*, published in the *Providence Journal*: "The theater was run by the people that also ran the Comique in Providence. It was making good money as the doors opened at 8 p.m. and closed at 3:00 a.m." He mentioned that as soon as the curtain went up, the girls rushed to the boxes, selling small bottles of champagne for five dollars. Dow also reported that mining was suspended on Sundays, so the theaters arranged extra amusements to extend the hours, offering dogfights, horse races and shooting matches.

Kemp became busy with his mine interests and leased the building to Billy Nuttall. On January 28, 1879, there was a farewell performance for Kemp of *A Trip Around the World*, with some of Kemp's favorite performers participating: actor Eddie Foy, dancer Harry Le Petite Sprague, violinist Dick Robinson, harp player Nellie, banjo player Lizzie Robinson, clog dancer Johnnie Connors and trapeze artist Mos. Leo.

William Nuttall was born in England in about 1833 and toured the United States as a comedian for a few years before opening Nuttal & Mann's Saloon in Deadwood. The saloon was a popular theater and gambling house. One would often find Wild Bill Hickok playing at one of the tables; he was shot and killed there on August 2, 1876. Nuttall was a superior businessman who knew that money was not made by the show but rather by the bar and waitresses. He heard money was being made in Leadville, so he moved his family here.

Billy Nuttall took over the theater on February 1, 1879, paying $1,750 per month in rent, while managing the Park Avenue Amphitheater. He remodeled the theater and added second-story rooms, housing many of the actors and earning back some of the money he paid them.

The theater had a gaming hall that was host to many bunko games. Nuttall was more interested in making money off the gaming tables than from the theater, and soon the Comique was known as the roughest gaming hall in Leadville. This became clear on July 2, 1879, when Officer Talbot was shot and killed while on duty in the Comique.

Nuttall donated the proceeds from the July production of *Pocahontas* to the widow Talbot and her children. The star of this performance was Gus Mills, a popular female impersonator, playing Pocahontas. When playing the female lead, Mills went by the pseudonym "Sarah Bernhardt." He played many leading lady roles at the Comique and later at the Grand Central Theater.

Eddie Foy was born in Greenwich Village, New York, on March 9, 1856. By the time he was six years old, he was performing in variety theaters and saloons to help support his family. As a young man, he traveled in the West, going from mining camp to mining camp. He came from Dodge City with actor Jim Thompson because they had a contract at the Comique. Foy said, "In many ways Leadville made Dodge City look like a Sunday School." Rooms were hard to come by, so Foy and Thompson, as well as a few other actors, bunked backstage on small, straw-filled mattresses. Foy was popular with the miners, and on many nights he was showered with coins after his performance; he also earned twenty-five dollars per week, paid by the house.

On July 27, 1878, Eddie's friends Jim Masterson (Bat Masterson's brother) and Wyatt Earp were in town and decided to go to the Comique and see their old friend. During the play, someone down the street started shooting, and some of the shots entered the theater wall. Masterson and Earp, standing near the front entrance, thought that it was an assassination attempt on them. Eddie described the incident as typical Leadville, explaining that these things went on all the time, and went back to finish the performance.

The Howland Sisters were playing at another theater, and although Eddie had met them when they were younger, he noticed how much Rose Howland had grown into a beautiful woman. Eddie and Rose began to see each other regularly, spending many evenings dining at the Tontine Restaurant.

Eddie and Rose were married on April 1, 1879, at the home of Pastor Thomas Uzzell, causing quite a stir with Rose's mother and sister. The marriage meant the end of the Howland Sisters' act; the sisters finished out the season, but then Rose joined Eddie on stage. Her mother and sister left Leadville and went back east.

In 1880, the Foys moved to Philadelphia, and while Rose was at home, getting ready for the birth of their first child, Eddie traveled around, looking for work. One day, he had a bad feeling and immediately returned home. Rose was in labor, but it did not go well. She died in Eddie's arms, and the baby did not survive.

Eddie met Lola Sefton in San Francisco, and they became a couple until her death. (Many sources describe them as husband and wife, although no marriage record has been found.) Ten years later, in 1896, he married Madeline Morando; they had eleven children, with seven living to adulthood. He returned to Leadville for brief visits in 1888 and 1900 to play at the Tabor Opera House.

In 1910, he formed a vaudeville act called "Eddie Foy and the Seven Little Foys." They played in a series of skits, with Eddie as the proud papa. Eddie took the act on the road, and it was a big hit for more than a decade. Madeline died in 1918, and in 1923, Eddie married Mary Coombs. He continued to act and travel until his death on February 16, 1928. *The Seven Little Foys* was a hit movie in 1955, with Bob Hope playing the part of Eddie Foy.

By 1879, the Comique was drawing a rough crowd; one reason was that the building was a mix of theater and gambling hall. One night in June, Officer Raines was working at the Comique, wearing his police uniform and taking tickets at the door. "Keno" Bill, an unsavory gambler, walked past the officer without paying admission. Raines was having none of this and called after Bill that he needed a ticket. Bill shouted back, "Hell I do!" Raines forcibly removed Bill from the building, assuming that this was the end of the incident.

At closing, a woman asked Raines to escort her home because she was afraid that the man outside might harm her. He escorted the woman home, and on his way back, two men approached him with guns drawn—one was "Keno" Bill. The other accused Officer Raines of running with his wife, so Raines blew his whistle for help. Bill stepped back and fired a shot; the bullet went through Raines's hat, grazing his forehead. Raines fired two shots, hoping that he would hit one, but "Keno" Bill was never seen in Leadville again. For several weeks, Raines and his hat were more popular than the show at the Comique; people stopped in to see the hat and hear how he survived a bullet to the head.

There was a little side room on the ground floor, off the saloon, that was referred to as "the joint"; it was a private gambling room. In 1879, Charles "Doc" Baggs, a local con man, played bunko here. Bunko is a dice game played with three dice, and the winning hand was three-of-a-kind.

Baggs was known as a bunko steerer, meaning that he steered the game his way. Legend says that he was arrested a thousand times in his life but never convicted. Once, when he was arrested and accused of bunko steering, he represented himself in the trial, stating that "there are no such words as bunko steering in the law books." He took out a dictionary, opened it and said that since he could not find "bunko steering" in there, how could such a crime exist? Dumbfounded, the judge dropped all charges, and Baggs walked away.

During Billy Nuttall's management, the Comique was quite successful and made a handsome profit. In 1879, Nuttall returned the keys to Tomas

Kemp, who closed the theater for a short period and reopened it as a concert hall in October. This lasted for eight days. In November, the Comique was torn down. The following month, Thomas Kemp built another theater, the Grand Central Theater, on the same site.

Wood's Opera House

Ben Wood came to Leadville in 1878 and purchased the Chestnut Street Theater at 103–105 East Chestnut Street. He remodeled the building, opening Leadville's first legitimate theater. Compared to earlier theaters that operated more as variety halls, this theater produced full-length plays. Wood remodeled the theater and changed the name to Wood's Opera House. When Wood reopened this theater, it had one thousand seats, fourteen boxes and Brussels carpet throughout, and the stage was forty-eight by one hundred feet. The scenes were painted on flat slides that were rolled in and out; flying curtains were not used. On opening night, October 13, 1879, a reporter for the *Herald Democrat* noted that "the actresses were wearing washed clothes." The theater was ahead of its time; gentlemen were not permitted to smoke or drink in the presence of a lady. Men were required to remove their hats and keep their boots on the floor—not resting on the back of the seats—to show the decorum required of a first-class theater. Less than a year later, Wood opened the Windsor Hotel next door.

Opening-night performers included those by Charles Vivian, Annie Bradden, Pauline Ames, Baby McDonald and Pebo the Dog. Billy Arlington also performed here, holding the audience spellbound with his jokes. Wood's Opera House was the first theater to put on *Uncle Tom's Cabin*, later played on every stage in Leadville.

Wood had a unique way of advertising performances. He had a large dog and attached a sandwich board sign to him, letting him run through town. One morning, while making his rounds, the dog collided with a team of

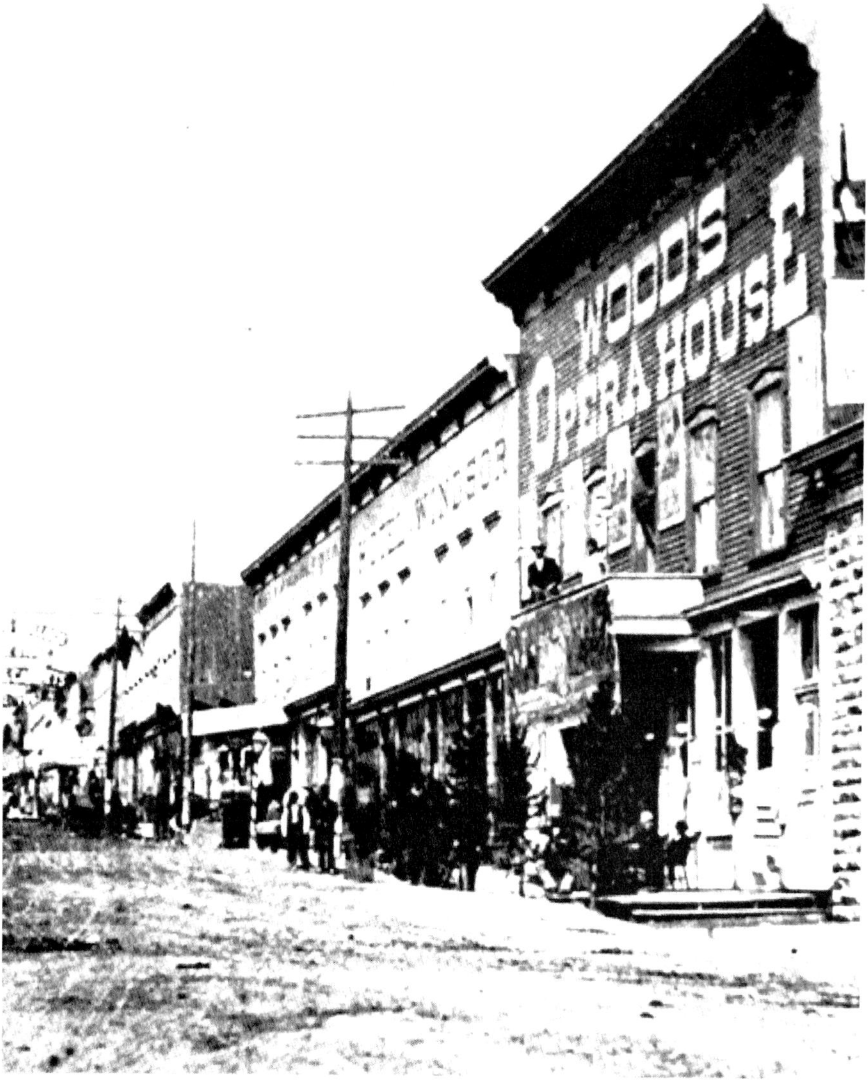

The Wood's Opera House in about 1878. *Courtesy of the Lake County Public Library Photo Collection.*

horses pulling the Coliseum advertising wagon. There was a band riding on the back, and the drummer boy was dumped from the wagon. The horses spooked and took off down the avenue, with the band in tow, finally stopping in Stringtown. It gave the crowd quite the show. The dog and horses were not hurt.

During Wood's ownership, Charles Vivian performed here in *Oliver Twist*. Vivian played the lead, and his wife, dressed as a boy, played Artful Dodger. Billy Nuttall, Leadville's favorite comic, also graced the stage before going to the Comique. Wood's Opera House was regarded as the largest and best theater ever constructed in the West—an honor it held for over a month, until the opening of the Tabor Opera House.

The Olympic Theater

Days after the opening of the Tabor Opera House, Ben Wood leased Wood's Opera House to A.E. Jones, who changed the name to the Olympic Theater. Opening night was November 25, 1879, with May Winters as the star in *Pocahontas*. This was not your Disney or historic view of the Indian maiden but rather a burlesque performance with skimpy, form-fitting costumes and racy dialogue.

Joseph Lowe, a gambling saloon owner, had loaned Jones the money to secure the lease, but he had not been receiving his payment on the $1,500 loan. On December 5, 1879, Mr. Lowe and a hired man went to the theater to demand payment. Jones tried to make excuses, saying that he had been to Lowe's Saloon three times to pay but that Lowe refused to see him. When the men arrived at the theater, they saw Jones counting money behind the counter, and Lowe demanded he stop; instead Jones tried to grab the money up and run. They grabbed him by the collar and threw him out on the street, along with his wife, their belongings and the theater manager. Jones tried to get back in by breaking a door, but to no avail. Jones, his wife and the manager took rooms at the Windsor Hotel, called the marshal and filed a warrant against Lowe.

That night, Lowe went to the theater and told everyone, "The show must go on." The actors didn't take kindly to the new management and refused to perform. A large house had packed the theater; they waited for two hours, becoming more and more restless. Finally, the orchestra played a few songs and exited the stage; it was announced that the show had been canceled. The crowd went wild; men demanded their money back, but the box office was closed, so guards ushered the angry crowd out and locked the doors.

The next day, all the parties were in court to answer charges. When Lowe found that he was being charged with a crime, he filed charges against Jones for vandalism to the door, adding $550 to the amount owed. Lowe defended the charges against him, saying that he did not forcibly take possession of the building. Since he held the mortgage, he felt he had joint possession of the building.

Jones came to court with $1,500, but Lowe refused to accept the money, insisting he was owed $2,450 ($1,500 on the chattel mortgage, $450 for a piano Jones purchased and $550 for the door). The judge found that Lowe was within his rights to hold the theater until payment was made. Jones approached fellow theater owner H.A.W. Tabor for a loan to repay Lowe. Tabor and Mr. Cooper, another business owner, loaned him the money, and performances resumed under the management of A.E. Jones.

For a few weeks, things seemed to be going smoothly, but Mr. Jones had other plans. On January 2, 1880, after a very successful New Years Eve, Jones loaded everything that was not nailed down into a wagon and left town in the dark of night. The next morning, the employees arrived at the theater and found the place locked. Jones owed a lot of people but left town without paying. Ben Wood paid off all the debts and hired Edwin Browne to manage the theater. It was renamed the Chestnut Street Theater and was reopened on January 12, 1880.

Chestnut Street Theater

In 1881, "Baby" McDonald was one of the lead acts in the stock company at this theater; she was born Mary McDonald in 1868. Her father, James, was a skater and dancer and introduced her to the stage at the age of three. Baby was very small and delicate-looking and lit up the stage with each performance, not only at the Chestnut Street but also later at Grand Central, McDaniel's, Ben Loeb's and Mike Goldsmith's Theaters. No matter which stage, she was one of Leadville's most popular hits.

At the age of thirteen, Baby decided that she was old enough to marry. Newspapers reported that she had many admirers who would have been

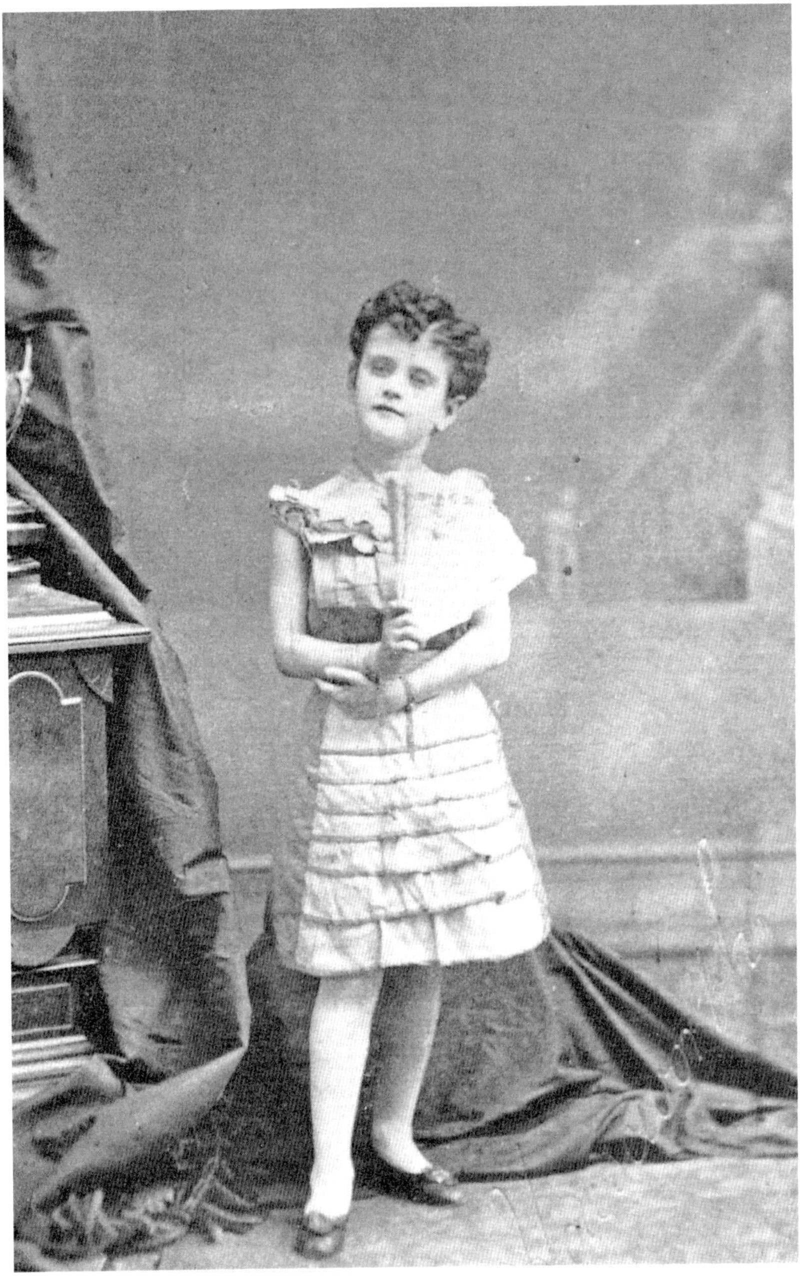

Baby McDonald photo taken in Deadwood, South Dakota, before she and her family moved to Leadville.

ecstatic had she chosen them. She picked A.E. Lewis, and one Sunday afternoon, the two ran off to the justice of the peace and were married. Baby's parents were outraged and began to look for Mr. Lewis. He feared that they would steal his new bride, so he locked her up in his house. Mrs. McDonald managed to find Mr. Lewis and poked him in the face with a shotgun, saying, "Baby or Brains." Lewis valued his brains more than his Baby, for he told Mrs. McDonald where to find her daughter. A divorce was filed, and Lewis was charged with assault and battery for keeping Baby locked away. Baby was called to testify and asked if she was going to live with her husband; she replied, "I guess not. I'm going back with my momma." Lewis was glad to be out of the marriage with only a small fine.

Baby McDonald's father had his own share of trouble while in Cincinnati, Ohio. He was accused of stabbing a man; when the man died, McDonald was tried for murder but acquitted. In June 1881, he decided to borrow a buggy (he may or may not have had permission) to take the theater children for a ride around Leadville. When McDonald returned to town, City Alderman John McComb, the buggy's owner, paying no mind to the children in the buggy, shot McDonald in the head. James died a few days later.

In 1884, Baby again eloped, this time with Alexander Martin, a young miner. Her mother was outraged and tried again to end the marriage by threatening Alexander with a shotgun. The couple moved to Robinson, a mining town just outside Leadville, near the Climax mine. The marriage didn't last long—in the winter of 1885, the couple had a fight. Baby left home in middle of the night, in a blinding snowstorm, and walked thirteen miles to Leadville. Her mother again helped her secure a divorce.

Baby returned to the stage, this time touring the country with a traveling troupe. She returned to Leadville and played at the Tabor Opera House in May 1887. Baby was in Providence, Rhode Island, in June 1892, and one night she was having trouble sleeping and decided to read for a while. She lit the lamp in her hotel room and dropped a match, which caught her nightgown on fire. The fire spread quickly, causing lethal burns. Although the hotelier smothered the flames with a blanket, she died five hours later.

Academy of Music

On January 22, 1881, Charlie Howard and Ned Sullivan leased the old opera house and closed the doors for remodeling. They hired architect Harry W. Barbour and removed the second floor, opening an area for seating in the new balcony. Also hired was George Heiman, a scene designer from Madison Square Theater in New York, who designed the scenes and the proscenium arch. The opera house was opened with a horseshoe gallery, a fly gallery, upholstered crimson red sofa benches, dressing rooms, new scenes, a new balcony and a new name, the Academy of Music. Opening night was March 21, 1881, and the show was *Arrah-na-Pogue.* Special scenery and a mechanical ivy tower were designed for the play.

Arrah-na-Pogue was the second of Dion Boucicault's great Irish plays, written after *Colleen Bawn* and before *Shaughraun*—all three were extremely popular in Leadville. The audience gasped at the climax of the play when Shaun, played by E.P. Sullivan, climbed up the ivy tower to be with his love, Arrah.

Sullivan and Howard were able to charge top rates for this performance: parquets and dress circle seats were one dollar, balcony circle seats were fifty cents and gallery seats were twenty-five cents. During their ownership, Howard and Sullivan were known to do things on a big scale; their reputation alone packed the house.

John Devoy was an Irish rebel, released from prison and exiled to America in 1861. He traveled across America, gaining support and money for Irish freedom. He packed the house; some stood on the street just to hear a little of what was said. He spoke at the Academy of Music in April 1881 and talked about the wrongs done to the Irish people. Leadville had a large Irish population, and when he passed the hat to help their relatives, the coffers overflowed.

In August, Sullivan discovered a fire between the walls of the empty cigar store attached to the theater and quickly ran for the fire extinguishers. When the fire was out, it was clear upon examination that someone had soaked the walls with coal oil, stuffed rags in a box of wood shavings and hidden the box under the building. The damage was repaired, but it was evident that there was an arsonist in Leadville. This fire was blamed on the same arsonist that had set the earlier Coliseum fire; he was never caught.

The show houses around town could no longer fill the seats; as a result, they paid lower salaries. In 1880, an actor made thirty-five dollars per week;

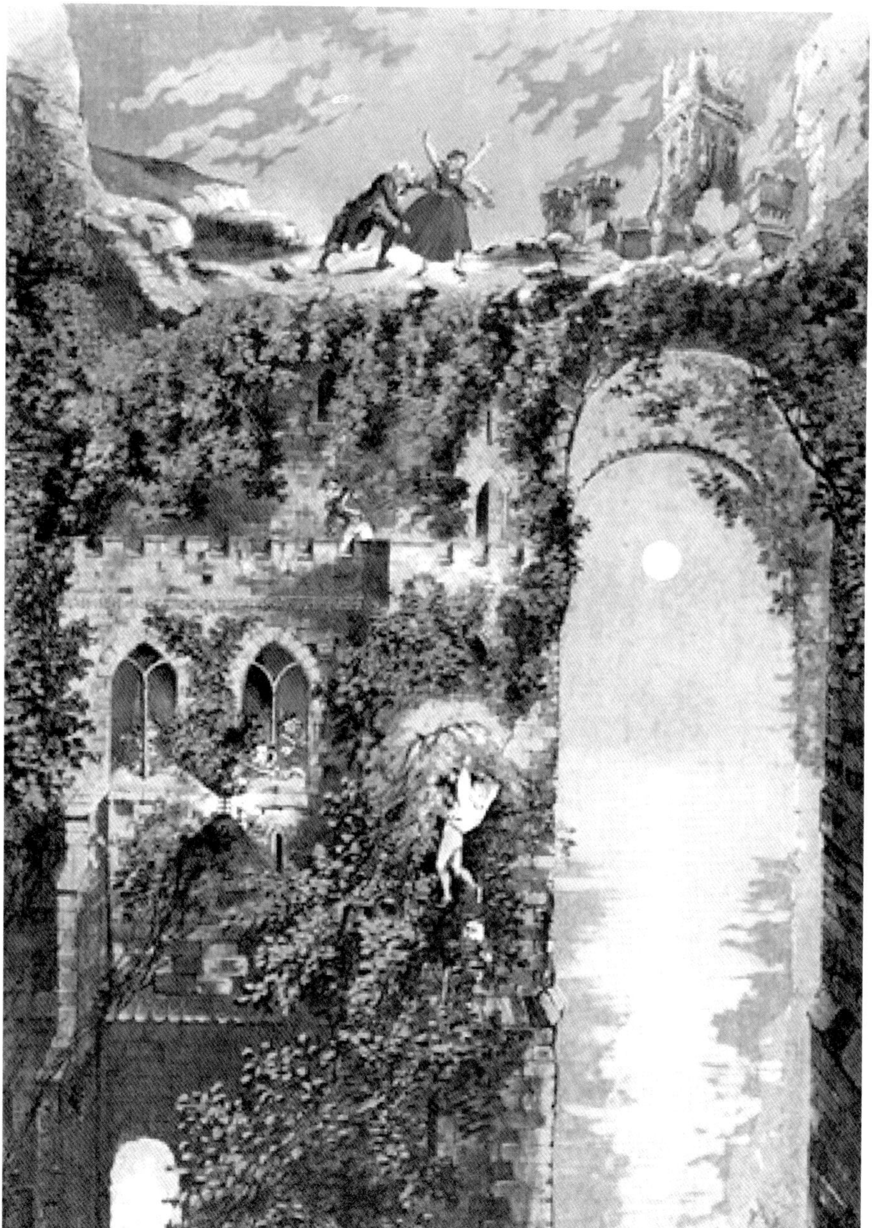

Poster from *Arrah-na-Pogue* similar to what may have been used to advertise the play in Leadville.

by 1881, that salary had been reduced to fifteen dollars. Many of the better actors left to follow the money. Shortly after the fire, Howard and Sullivan closed the doors. The *Herald Democrat* reported that "it has been an unlucky place from the day of its opening."

On May 19, 1882, shouts of "Fire! Fire!" were heard on East Chestnut Street. When people rushed out to the street, they noticed that the Palace of Fashion was fully engulfed. Flames spread quickly to the Hotel Windsor, and ladders were raised to rescue those trapped on the second floor. The wind blew the fire onto the Hotel Brunswick, and soon it was a pile of ashes. Some of the firemen who successfully put out the fire in the liquor store warehouse began sampling the wares, passing them around among themselves. Things quickly got out of hand when one of the firemen spotted a friend in the crowd. As a greeting, he took one of the hoses off the fire and drenched the crowd.

Newly elected alderman C.C. Joy was surveying the damage and noticed this behavior, shouting at the firemen and calling them "drunken sons of bitches." Andrew King, a volunteer fireman, did not take kindly to the name-calling and gave Mr. Joy a shove. Joy swung back, and quickly spectators and fireman joined in the fight. Unfortunately, while the brawl was going on, the winds picked up and carried the flames to the Academy of Music.

The heat was so intense that the firemen abandoned their firefighting efforts on those buildings and began working farther up the street, saving what they could. While working to save the First National Bank, the firemen lost water pressure and had to shut off half the hoses, though they did save the bank building. Finally, the firemen were able to get control of the fire and save the rest of the buildings. Damages were estimated at more than $500,000, along with one death—the badly burned body of Arthur Ballou, a businessman staying at a hotel, turned up.

The community was shocked to learn that the cause of the fire was arson. Police quickly arrested Fred Butler, owner of the Palace of Fashion, along with his employees Isaac Kamak, Reuben Weil, Maurice Zippert and Reinhold Rosendorf, a barber. The original theory was that the fire was set to claim the insurance; however, this was a successful store, and it was not fully insured for the value lost.

At the trial in March 1883, a statement was read from Jack Brogan, an inmate in the Canon City Penitentiary who was serving time for setting fire to the Famous Shoe Store a few months after the Chestnut Street fire. Brogan was also accused of setting a few other fires around town. In the statement, Brogan said that he was a volunteer fireman at the Central Fire

Station when two men, Bryce Blair and Walter Wilson, came to him and invited him to a dance. They headed over to the Palace of Fashion, and Blair and Wilson said that they were going to burn it down. Brogan stated that he stood watch but did not set the fire. Blair and Wilson left town shortly thereafter. The jury came back with an acquittal of all parties. Jack Brogan was released from prison in 1884.

The Park Avenue Amphitheater

The Park Avenue Amphitheater was a tent-covered building on West Fifth Street between Park and Lafayette Avenues that Billy Nuttall used as a theater. It was constructed in 1879 by Tom Day and Jim Anderson and could seat two thousand people. It had a very short history—it is said that people in Leadville would not go to the theater in a tent. Nuttall was a veteran theater man who had managed the Bella Union Theater in Deadwood, South Dakota, before he arrived in Leadville.

He managed the theater for a short period but found the size of the Amphitheater overwhelming and leased it to Joseph Proctor. Proctor operated it for a few days—playing in *Nick o' the Woods*, *Jack Cade* and *Richelieu*—before forfeiting the lease. Nuttall then leased the theater to Charles Vivian, the most well-known comedian of the American stage at the time.

Vivian's Opera House

Charles Algernon Sidney Vivian was born in Devonshire County, England, on October 22, 1842. After his father's death, Charles developed a talent for acting, playing on local stages. He immigrated to New York on November 15, 1867, and began performing as a singer and comedian.

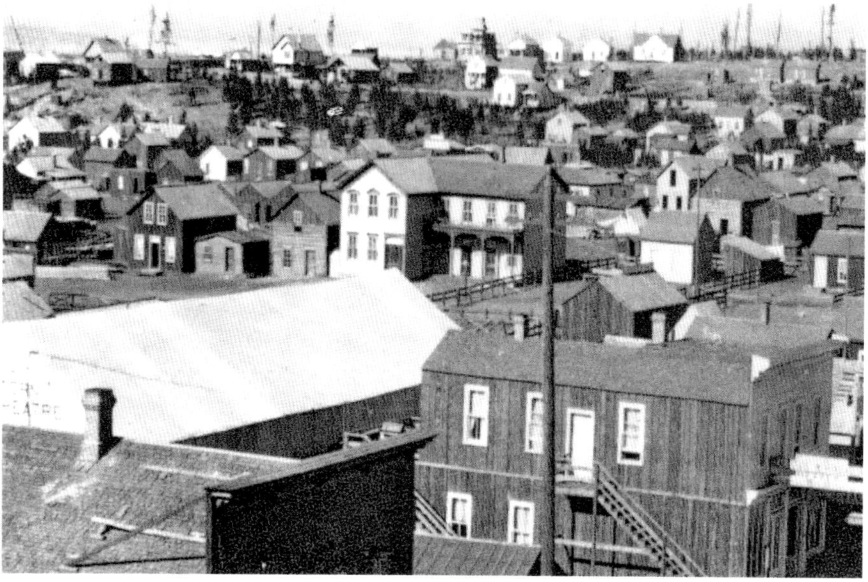

Photo of the Park Avenue Amphitheater in about 1879. *Courtesy of the Colorado Mountain History Collection, Lake County Public Library.*

Charles socialized with a group of friends in the same profession, and they founded the Jolly Corks Society; Vivian was chosen as the first Imperial Cork. The name is said to have derived from a bar game Vivian played in England. The group was a fun-loving, loose-knit drinking group organized to avoid New York's laws prohibiting the sale of alcohol on Sunday. Only clubs and fraternal organizations were exempt and could sell alcoholic beverages on Sundays to their members. When one Jolly Corks member died and his wife had no money to bury him, the group began a new mission as a benevolent society. The name was changed to the Benevolent Protection Order and later to the Benevolent Protection Order of the Elks. Charles Vivian voted against changing the name to the Elks, wishing instead to change the name to the Buffalos.

Vivian was quite popular on the stages of San Francisco and had a large following. There he met Imogene Holbrook, an actress from the same company. They fell in love. Charles told her it was love at first sight and proposed marriage. The two were married on July 9, 1876, in Oakland, California. Shortly after the wedding, they traveled to mining towns in

Montana, Nevada and Utah and then to the East Coast before coming west again. Eventually, the company made its way to Denver and played in *Pinafore* and *Trial by Jury*.

After those performances, the company disbanded, and Vivian decided to go to Leadville and do a little "prospecting" in the theatrical line. He joined a party headed that way; the trip was difficult since the railroad had not yet reached Leadville. Leaving his wife in Denver, he set off for "the camp where Dame Fortune with her magic touch smiled sweetly upon the minority," according to his wife.

A week after he arrived, Charles sent for Imogene; he had secured a lease on the Amphitheater and renamed it the Vivian Opera House, offering the type of entertainment that women would not be afraid to attend and to which they could take their children. Imogene said that the managers of other theaters were only interested in catering to the rough elements, and their desire was to fill their coffers rather than present legitimate drama.

The theater drew a crowd at the box office; however, once they realized that there was no liquor or smoking, many walked away. The first show, on August 25, was *Dora*. It received rave reviews, many noting that no better theater group could be found anywhere in Leadville. Every show that was performed under Vivian's management received rave reviews, but it didn't keep the Vivian open. By September 1, the Vivian had closed, due to the prohibitions against smoking and drinking in the theater and also because Leadville did not have the climate for a theater in a tent.

Vivian moved on to other theaters, working at the Comique and the Wood's Opera House. While at Wood's, the advertising noted, "Come, see The Only Vivian." One newspaper pointed out that there was another man in Leadville by the name of Vivian; one morning, he was seen standing by a poster saying, "Well, if that is the only Vivian, who the devil am I?" Vivian left Wood's Opera House after he contracted a severe cold that affected his voice. For a short time, he became a reviewer of theater for the *Chronicle*.

One evening, after attending a dinner party, he turned to his wife and said, "My dear, I shall never leave Leadville alive." This prophecy was fulfilled a short time later when he fell gravely ill while entertaining friends at a clubhouse. They sent for his wife, believing that he was so sick they could not move him. A few hours later, Imogene got a carriage and moved him to their rented rooms. With the help of doctors and friends, she tried to nurse him back to health, but he died seven days later with his wife beside him.

Charles was buried the next day, on March 21, 1880, at Evergreen Cemetery. The funeral was arranged by the Pacific Coast Association and held at the Tabor Opera House. The casket was escorted to the cemetery by the Knights of Pythias, the Merchant Police and the Pacific Coast Association. His grave was marked with a simple wooden marker.

In 1888, James Green, a bartender at Loeb's Palace of Pleasure, began making a fuss about the condition of Vivian's and other actors' graves at Evergreen Cemetery. Thomas Daly was playing at the Tabor Opera House, and Green told him of the terrible shape of Vivian's grave and took him on a tour of the cemetery. Daly contacted the Elks in Boston and told them of the state of things. The Boston lodge was outraged and came to Leadville to see the condition firsthand. They decided that the founder of the Elks needed a grander monument than a wooden headstone and made plans to move the body to Boston.

Dr. Law, a family friend, contacted Mrs. Vivian to tell her of the plans to move her husband. The Boston lodge had not contacted her and did not have her permission to remove her husband from his place of rest; however, the telegram arrived the day his remains were removed. Mrs. Vivian tried to get the police to intervene, but to no avail. Despite her objections, his remains were transferred by train to Boston on April 22, 1889.

Palace of Buckingham

After Charles Vivian's death, Nuttall leased the theater to the Tudor family; for a few short weeks, they called it Tudor's Place. Next, it was renovated into a dance hall named the Palace of Buckingham. The hall that was opened in November 1880, leased by Mr. Rees and Mr. Taylor, was known to be a hangout for loose women. A newspaper classified ad read, "Missed you at the dance at the Palace of Buckingham last Thursday. Hope to see you there this Tuesday, Carrie." These classifieds ran every week, apparently as an enticement from "Carrie's House," a local house of prostitution.

On January 13, 1881, an alarm sounded at the firehouse indicating that the Tabor Opera House was on fire, but when fire crews arrived, they couldn't find any fire. Someone began yelling that the Buckingham was burning; crews ran over and found that the tent had fallen down in the wind, trapping three men inside. Jinks Taylor, the bartender, was trapped under heavy timber and badly injured; the other two were able to walk out. When questioned, they stated that they were upstairs at the bar when they heard a loud crack, and minutes later, the wind blew the building down. The cause was attributed to high winds and large snowfall.

Billy Nuttall stated that he would rebuild the theater. In March, the work crew had begun clearing away the rubble when one of the workers discovered a trapdoor to the wine room. When the door was opened, the workers found that it was just a large, deep pit. A worker was lowered into the pit and swore that a body was down there. Further investigation uncovered the bodies of several unidentified persons; attempts were made to identify them, but to no avail. Rumors began to fly that Tom Day and Jim Anderson, the builders, had used the pit to dispose of men they had robbed and killed. They had a reputation for robbing patrons at the theater and had been chased out of town by a vigilante committee. The building was renovated and reopened as the Buckingham Dance Hall on April 3, 1881.

The Turne-Halle

The Turnverein Society was an organization devoted to the practice of German gymnastics; members had to be of German descent. Turne-Halle was leased by the Turnverein Society in 1878 and was located on the northeast corner of Third and Poplar Streets (206–208 East Third Street). It was a large building, with the front section occupied by a saloon, and the second floor housed a spacious hall and several smaller rooms. It was used for a variety of affairs: literacy readings, gymnastic exercises, theatrical performances, dances and musical concerts. In the beginning, all performances—whether musical, theatrical or sport—were given in German. Later, as the organization grew, more performances were given in English.

Members dedicated hours of training into building their muscles to a more fit body, with classes given to German men of all ages. Instruction comprised exercise leaping, a vaulting horse, a rack of horizontal bars, parallel bars, a trapeze, rings, a round swing, a seesaw, a crossbeam, upright climbing poles, balancing clubs and horizontal climbing bars.

The first Leadville Assembly Balls were held here, the most lavish in the state. A fine dinner was enjoyed first, and afterward couples danced to the most popular music of the day, played by a large orchestra. The Assembly Balls were moved to the Clarendon Hotel when it opened in 1879. Mary Hallock Foote wrote *The Last Assembly Ball*, published in 1889, based on these events. In 1913, Denver began holding Assembly Balls at the Brown Palace Hotel, modeled after Leadville.

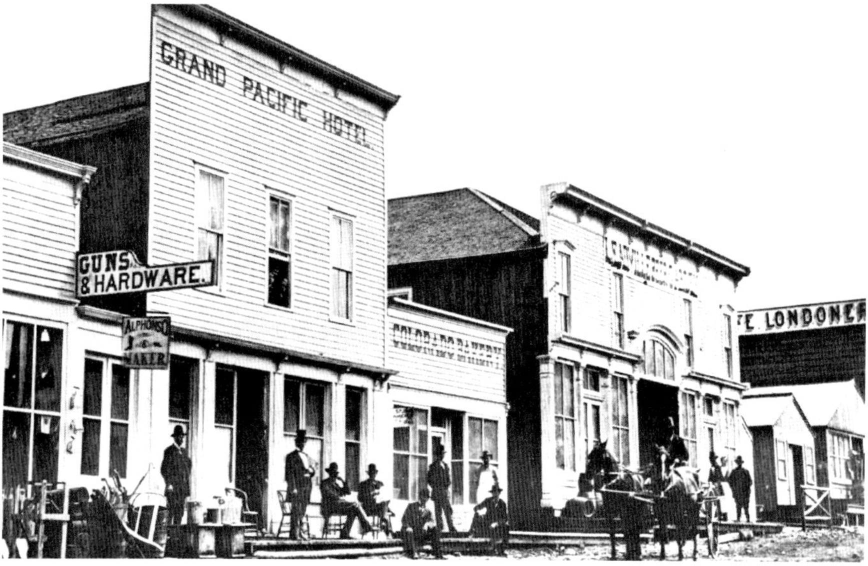

Photo of Turner Hall, circa 1879. *Courtesy of the Colorado Mountain History Collection, Lake County Public Library.*

There were only 12 members in 1878; by 1879, membership had grown to 180. The group became so large that it split into two groups, the West Turners and the East Turners.

East Turner Hall

In May 1887, Mr. Hoebel purchased the building, choosing to run the upstairs as a hall and leasing it to the Turners; the name remained East Turner Hall.

On February 27, 1888, the hall was packed to standing room only; all were there to show their support to the anti-prohibition supporters. Rob Blumenburg rallied the crowd by speaking in German about the danger of prohibition. He said that no one agreed with inebriation, but many German families could lose their jobs, homes and investments if prohibition became law. The Turners had been speaking out in opposition to any prohibition or temperance movement since March 1881, when they held their first anti-temperance rally.

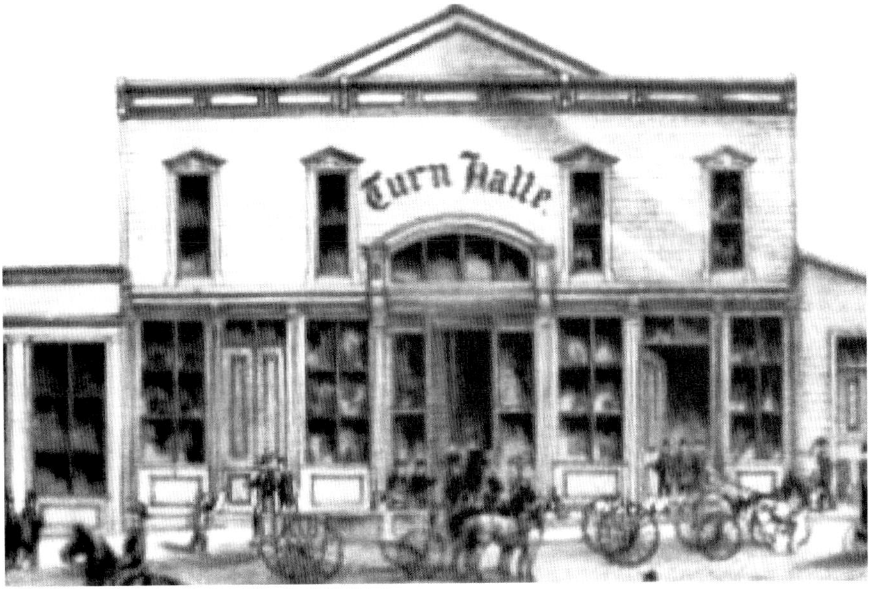

Line drawing of Turne-Halle, from the *Herald Democrat*.

Most prohibition rallies in Leadville were not well received. The representatives from the East and West groups were elected to lead the charge of a German anti-temperance organization, one of the first in Leadville. This group started a campaign to invite all like-minded people to join and save Colorado, including Leadville, from the fate they saw Kansas suffering from with its prohibition laws.

Leadville's first ski club was founded on January 11, 1914. The founders were expecting about ten to twelve people who would be interested in a club devoted to skiing. However, when the meeting opened at the office of J.G. Schali on East Fifth Street, so many people arrived that the meeting was moved to the hall. Most had never skied before but were eager to learn.

The first formal ski school was held a few days later at the Ibex mine. New equipment was brought from Denver on the train, as there was not enough in stock for all those who wanted to ski. The class started at the mine and proceeded down the hill until the students reached town.

In July 1915, the hall was closed for renovations. A new maple floor was laid throughout the gymnasium that was also used as a dance floor; the hall was rewired, painted and enlarged to include dressing rooms, making it the second-largest hall in the city (City Hall being the largest).

With Leadville's short summer season, some of the traditionally outdoor games had to be moved indoors; therefore, because of its size, the hall became the host for indoor baseball games. Although the field was a little smaller and foul balls bounced off the ceiling, the games were as exciting as any outdoor game. Afterward, both teams stayed for a dance.

New Turnverein or West Turner Hall

In 1880, the Turnvereins built their new hall (also known as the West Turner Hall) at West Fourth Street and the southeast corner of Pine; the cornerstone was laid on June 8. A large crowd paraded down the street to see the event, which included the police squad, the mayor and city council, the Vienna Ladies Orchestra Band, the Knights of Pythias, the Freemasons, the Odd Fellows, the Ancient Order of the Hibernians and Castello's Great American Circus.

M.J. Waldheimer addressed the crowd and talked eloquently of the origin of athletic sports, dating back to the days of Greece and Rome and later adopted into English customs. He said that the Germans developed the societies that combined athletic sports with social, mental and physical development to better prepare men for the hardships of war. Mayor Humphreys took the podium and talked about the importance of the German citizens to Leadville. At the end of the speech, the cornerstone was laid with great ceremony. It was a large building, complete with a spacious stage, several finely painted scenes, a cloakroom, two waiting rooms and a large dining room. The hall was used for many types of entertainment in addition to gymnastics. The Turners stayed until 1884, when they moved to 205 West Chestnut Street.

In 1881, a wrestling match packed the hall. It was a $500 match between F.W. Hilgert and Andre Christol. The local newspapers published the rules that wrestlers had to abide by.

1. *No hold shall be allowed lower than the waist.*
2. *The wrestling shall be with open hands.*
3. *No striking, scratching or gouging allowed.*
4. *There shall be restrictions in regard to grips, clasping of hands and interlacing of fingers being agreed upon.*
5. *The wrestlers must have their fingernails cut close, and they must wrestle in soft shoes or socks.*
6. *A fall shall be declared when either man has been fairly put upon his back, with the two shoulders on the ground at the same time.*
7. *In the event of the wrestlers rolling over each other, the one whose shoulders touch the ground first, as under rule 6, shall be deemed to have lost one fall.*
8. *Fifteen minutes rest shall be allowed between bouts, and either man failing to appear when time is called shall be considered to have lost the match.*
9. *This match shall be decided by either party to this agreeing winning two out of the three falls.*
10. *The judges shall examine the men between each bout to see that no oil or grease has been put upon their skin.*

Andre Christol was known as the "Champion Greco-Roman Wrestler," and he came to Leadville in March 1880 to arrange a match with Ed Cudihee, the "Collar and Elbow Champion." Cudihee later became the marshal of Leadville and leased the Grand Central Theater. He stayed in Leadville for a number of years, arranging boxing and wrestling matches.

After the Turners moved from this hall, it was leased to Louis Miller & Company, and it ran a small show house with dancing, band performances and theatrical entertainment. In August 1881, a few nights after the fire at the Academy of Music, the alarm again rang on the streets of Leadville. This time, it was the Old Turner Hall that was on fire. A passerby noticed a large amount of smoke pouring from the building and rang the alarm bell. Someone had started a fire at the northeast corner of the building, and the flames spread, lighting the oil canvases on the stage.

The fire department got the fire under control. Investigation showed that the walls had been soaked with coal oil. Thanks to the efforts of the fire department, the fine bar in the front was saved, as was the liquor supply. It was believed to have been the same arsonist who set fire to the Academy of Music and the Coliseum earlier that year. The damage was repaired, and it was reopened soon afterward.

Leadville Athletic Club

Long before the opening of the Leadville Athletic Club, boxing and wrestling matches were seen on the stage of the variety theaters and opera houses or at the Sportsman's Hall. Most of these bouts were fought between experienced fighters and amateurs looking to make a quick buck. Theater owners like Ben Loeb and James McDaniel were known for offering money to ordinary men willing to go a few rounds in the ring against experienced boxers.

The Leadville Athletic Club was founded on June 28, 1883, by a group of amateur athletes. Professor Donald Dinnie was hired to be the trainer; his salary was $5,000 per year. An order for new uniforms was sent to New York for twenty-four Highland costumes, which included Scottish caps, kilts, low shoes, short stockings and a waist made of gum cloth. The club also purchased new equipment such as horizon bars, dumbbells, Indian clubs, light and heavy hammers and shots. This club allowed ladies to join but only if they were single.

The hall was remodeled, with the main floor divided into three rooms. One contained the gymnasium and was used as a gym for boxing and wrestling. The second room housed a bowling alley, and the third had a piano, pool and billiard tables, as well as a large bar for refreshments. The second floor had meeting space and a ballroom and hosted occasional theatrical performances. Over the next few years, the hall continued to be rented to other clubs for their activities; it was commonly referred to as Old Turner Hall.

Leadville and the Athletic Club rolled out the red carpet for two hundred members of the National Traveling Passenger Agents Convention and their families. On August 15, 1884, members of the Athletic Club went to Buena Vista to greet them on the train. Then they boarded the train and traveled with them to Leadville. Upon arrival, they were greeted by a band playing and hundreds of people cheering; carriages took them to the Clarendon Hotel.

The next morning, members of the club took them on carriage rides to visit the mines and also out to Evergreen Lakes for the afternoon. In the evening, the agents and their families were the guests of honor at a grand ball. Elegantly inscribed invitations were sent out. Everyone in Leadville wanted to attend the grand affair.

A railroad track was laid at the entrance of the hall, and in the center of the track a red carpet led to the doors. A switch was placed on one side of the track, and on the other side Sam Cole, in a conductor's uniform, was holding a lantern. He punched everyone's invitation as they arrived. Elegant programs were given to the attendees; on the exterior was an embossed monogram of the association in blue, ermine and gold.

The walls were decorated with railroad place cards, timetables and illuminated railroad signs. The floor was covered with a large white canvas; electric lights cast a kaleidoscope of color across the white floor, and a huge Japanese umbrella hung from the ceiling. A large railroad clock hung on one wall, and around the center of the clock were the words "Railroad Time." At the end of the hall was an elk's head, with railroad hammers and fence foil placed in his antlers. The entire building was draped in flags, adding to the grandeur. The stage held the band, seated in a semicircle, around a cross that bore the name "George W. Cook." Above the stage, a large eagle was suspended, with outstretched wings, and in its beak was a shield with a picture of a locomotive. The band began playing at 9:00 p.m. and did not stop until midnight. Before the last dance, a representative of the agents took the stage and said, "We have never had a more royal reception and such a perfect ovation."

That night, Leadville showed how important the railroads were to this community. The ball and convention were considered successes, and both mining and businesses were sure that the agents would encourage their respective companies to route Colorado excursions through Leadville. A few weeks after the ball, a large framed painting arrived as a gift for the Athletic Club from the National Traveling Passenger Agents—a thank-you for the wonderful time they had. The painting was of the death of Lord Nelson at the Battle of Trafalgar.

In its early years, the club was one of the most popular in town, with more than two hundred members; sadly, by 1888, membership had dwindled and so had the focus on exercise. In November, it dropped the word "Athletic" from its name and became the Leadville Gentlemen's Club. It gave up its lease on the building and moved its headquarters to the second floor in the Carbonate Bank Building (Old Standard Hall) on the northwest corner of Harrison Avenue and West Fourth Street.

The Lyceum Theater

Mr. S.S. Simpson reopened the theater in 1895 under the name Lyceum Theater. Seats cost ten cents; it was closed on Tuesdays, and Sunday matinees were only for women and children. He had a strong, velvety voice that was greatly admired by the ladies. During his management, Simpson was usually cast as the leading man, with the other actors playing lesser roles around him. He employed local amateur actors and the occasional, lesser-known traveling performer.

By January 1896, the company was playing to empty houses; no matter how good the plays were, it could not fill the seats. Its biggest competitor was the Ice Palace. The company shut the doors and went on tour. During its absence, the theater was completely remodeled: benches were removed and replaced with stylish theater chairs, two-story boxes were added to the sides of the stage, the stage was elevated and the floor placed at an angle. The box office was also removed and a smoking parlor added.

Paddy Mack reopened the theater late in 1898 and leased it to the King Kimbell Komedy Kompany (the 4Ks). The stage and seating at the Lyceum were larger than most in Leadville, and this helped the 4Ks because it was very popular and frequently had to turn away customers. After the opening of the Lyceum, the City Hall ceased having nightly performances and even gave the Weston (Tabor) Opera House a great deal of competition.

Paddy Mack retired in July 1899, and the theater was leased to Leon Henry and H.A. Hagen. They continued to employee a stock company, with performances every night, and programs changed every three to four days; traveling theater acts were also booked. Thus, it directly competed with the Weston Opera House, which booked the hottest traveling shows, as well as offered cheaper admission.

A.W. Fremont and his stock company took over management in 1901. With the dispute over the ownership of the Weston Opera House and its subsequent closing, the Lyceum Theater received a packed house almost every day.

The Lyceum hosted its first boxing match on October 17, 1902, when Dago Mike, a local fighter, fought Cal Harris of Chicago for the 118-pound championship and a $250 prize. The theater had to add seats to the stage to hold the large crowds that these fights commanded; for this fight, even standing room was sold out. Spectators were disappointed when Cal took

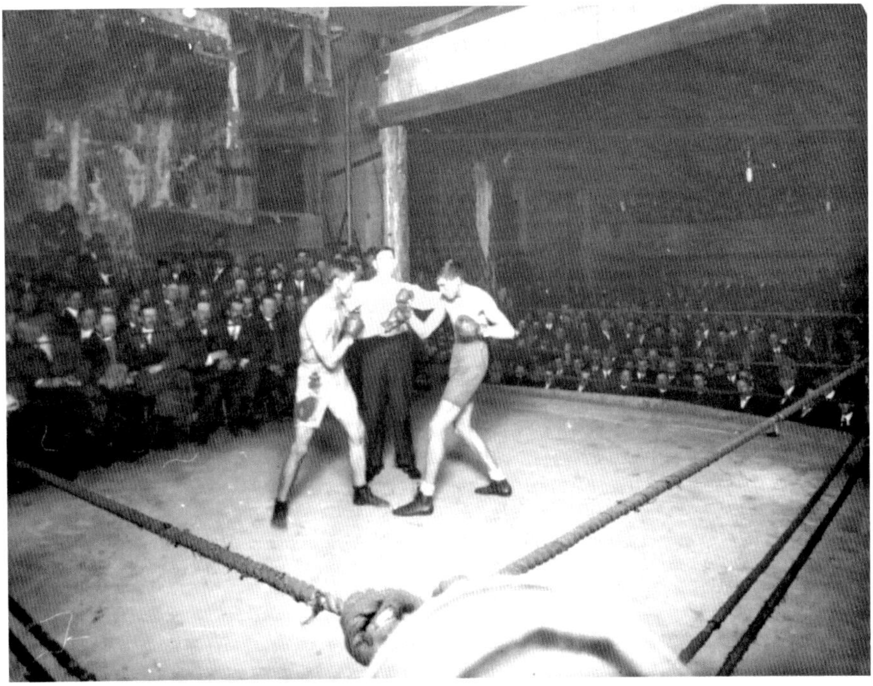

Prizefight in Leadville theater. *Courtesy of the Colorado Mountain History Collection, Lake County Public Library.*

the stage; the newspaper described him as "a mere skeleton that should have been in an invalid's chair on the consumption ward."

In the first round, it was easy to predict the winner. Dago danced circles around his opponent, jamming punches here and there and dodging everything Cal sent his way. Within seconds of the second round, Dago threw a right swing that landed on Cal's jaw. This laid Cal out on the floor; Dago carried him to his corner. When the fight was called, Cal stumbled over to shake Dago's hand.

By 1903, the theater could no longer compete and finally closed the doors. Later, Clyde Heller used the building as a garage. In May 1917, there was an unusually large snowfall, two feet in a few hours. The roof caved in under an estimated fifteen tons of weight, taking with it the south wall. Mr. Heller had no insurance, and the building was torn down.

The Shoenberg Opera House

The Shoenberg Opera House, at 205 West Chestnut on the corner of Pine, was owned by the Moses Shoenberg family; Moses later became David May's partner. The opera house was located on the second floor of a wood-frame building. It was not elaborate, and it had rough wood chairs and rows of uneven benches. The opera house was also used as a temple for the Jewish people of Leadville.

This opera house had a short history, opening on February 13, 1879, with a special presentation of *The Honeymoon* and *The Rough Diamond* by the Forrester Dramatic Group, a stock company. Nat Forrester and his wife, the leading performers, were originally part of Jack Langrishe's traveling troupe. H.A.W. Tabor and members of his hose company were in the audience that evening.

Soon afterward, notices appeared in the newspaper for nonpayment of bills. The Foresters left Leadville in March. In April, a notice appeared in the newspaper stating that "unless more patrons visited the legitimate opera houses, instead of variety theaters, the Shoenberg Opera House would be forced to close."

The most memorable group to play at the Shoenberg was the Hutchinson family singers, under the name Tribe of Asa, in June 1879. They were a traveling theater group that had been performing for more than two generations by the time they reached Leadville, and they were famous for their sweet melodies about the Civil War. The Hutchinson family also played at the Tabor Opera House in September 1880.

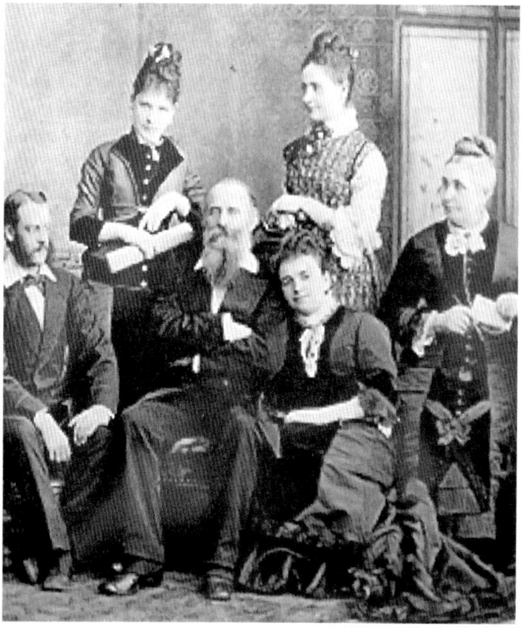

The Hutchinson family.

Asa Hutchinson relocated his family to Leadville, where he purchased the St. Julian Hotel and Restaurant. The restaurant was successful, and they entertained their guests with songs while they dined. In August 1879, one of the waiters at the restaurant refused to serve a black man. When Asa heard about this, he and his son, Oliver, served the man themselves. Asa was an abolitionist as well as a suffragist; his daughter, Abby, and her husband also become very strong participants in both movements in their later years. Word got around about the incident, and sales at the restaurant declined, forcing Asa to sell it.

The family continued to make their home in Leadville in a house located on Fourth Street, where they were known to give many musical parties. Years before coming to Leadville, Asa's wife had died, leaving him a widower until he married his second wife, Joanna. When Asa became ill in 1881, they left Leadville and traveled back to Minnesota. In 1882, Asa and Joanna returned to Leadville and turned their home into the Hotel Hutchinson.

After Asa's death, Joanne leased the Clarendon Hotel and became involved in the everyday management. In 1885, Joanna took over the Tabor Grand Hotel and married G.W. Bittinger. This caused quite a scandal because Mr. Bittinger had promised to wed Miss Lizzie Kline; she sued for breach of contract for $10,000.

When Asa died in 1884, he left the home to his son, Oliver Denton Hutchison. Joanna believed that the home should have been hers and sued Oliver. She lost that battle in 1887, and the home remained in Oliver's hands.

The Shoenberg Opera House was unable to compete with the larger and grander Tabor Opera House, which had opened in November 1879. The county commissioners purchased the building in January 1880 and used it as the courthouse until March, when a new courthouse was built. The building was still used for overflow courtrooms until 1883, when the county sold it to the Turners.

New Turner Hall

In 1884, the Turners changed the name of the building to the New Turner Hall and remodeled it to fit their needs; however, they had a hard time competing with the much larger East Turner Hall. Soon, the stage was rented for some of the more gruesome shows that Leadville offered—dogfights and cockfights. These fights were accepted and celebrated events.

On March 28, 1888, Denver senator Jack Finn's dog, Dollar, took on Jim Burke's dog, Bode. Both were pretty evenly matched at twenty-four pounds, but Bode had the advantage because Dollar had injured his leg in an earlier fight. In the second round, Bode refused to fight and had to be forced back into the ring. Dollar was more aggressive. When the third round ended, the decision was given to him. As the winner, his owner received $25. After the fight, Dollar's owner challenged any dog in Colorado to fight for prizes ranging from $100 to $500.

By 1888, the building had fallen into disrepair, and the Turners sold it. For several years, it was used as a wholesale butcher shop.

Grand Central Theater

Thomas Kemp tore down the Comique Theater to build the Grand Central Theater in order to build a bigger, more stable structure and draw larger crowds. The new theater, of brick and frame, was 75 by 135 feet; the stage was 35 by 55 feet, and the auditorium was 55 by 100 feet. The entrance was flush with the sidewalk and had a large veranda that allowed a band to play to the crowd below. Two huge columns held up the roof, and the entrance opened to a triangular alcove that led to the box office and bar.

The theater was located behind two large double doors opening into an auditorium that seated 1,500 people. Tables and chairs were in front of the stage so patrons could partake of refreshments during the play. The large stage curtain measured twenty-six by twenty-seven feet. It had one of the most complete stages, with fifty-five sets of scenes, speaking tubes, a set of bells and four trapdoors in the stage floor. Five dressing rooms and a property room were located under the stage.

The staircase in the entryway accessed the second floor via a carpeted promenade from which one could see the stage and auditorium below. At the end was a piano and mahogany bar; on the other side was the manager's office. Off the promenade were several wine rooms, stocked with the best refreshments and served by beautiful waitresses. Seven boxes were outfitted with electric bells to summon the waitresses. The boxes had white muslin curtains at the back, hung so that the occupants could see the stage but not be seen by anyone in the theater. The third floor had seating for an

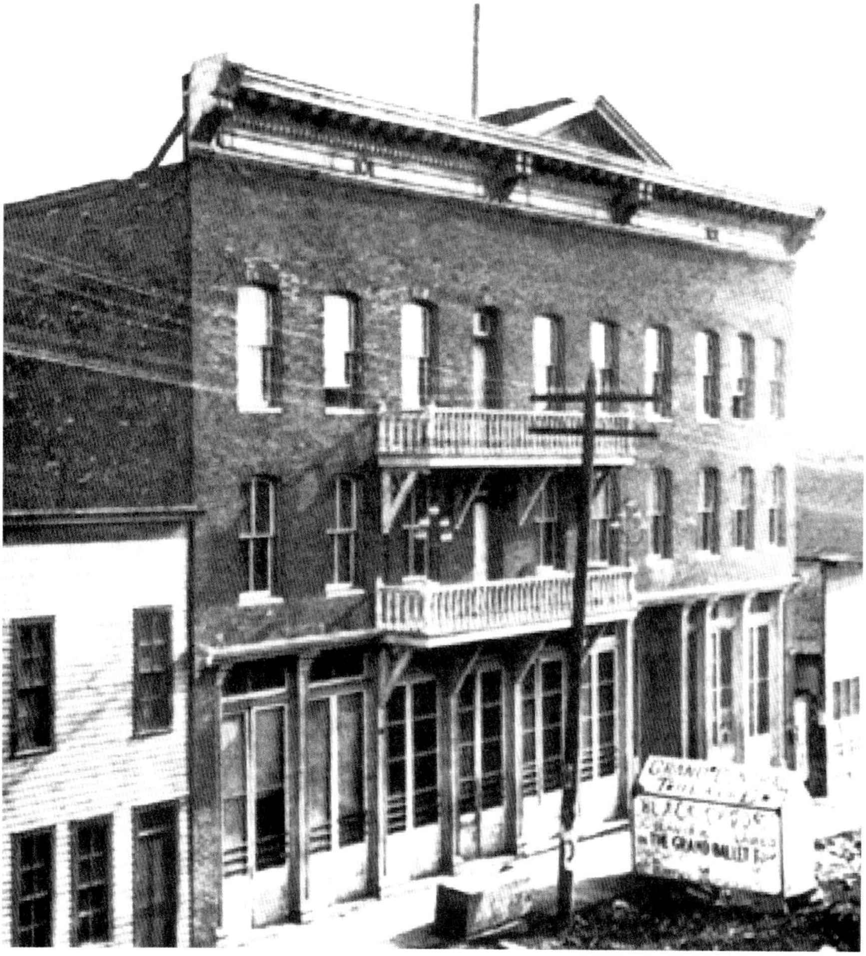

Grand Central Theater, 1880. *Courtesy of the Colorado Mountain History Collection, Lake County Public Library.*

additional 750 people. The theater also had thirty sleeping rooms located on the third floor.

The Grand Central Theater was hailed as the grandest theater in the West, lit by 255 brilliant gaslights. At the time of construction, it was the largest in the state, and although it was grander and larger than the Tabor Opera House, it cost less to build—$52,000 (in brick and wood) compared to $75,000 (in brick and stone) for the Tabor Opera House.

When it was built, many said that the theater would never be a financial success and called it a "white elephant." This turned out to be true. Due to the large size, it was costly to heat, staff and operate. Although many of the owners, managers and leasers promised to make this a legitimate theater, it never rose above its burlesques nature. This may have been in part due to location. State Street was known as the "Wickedest Place on Earth"; a proper lady would never venture onto State Street, not even to see the greatest show on earth. Despite the reputation, some great actors and actresses played here and went on to famous careers in New York, Chicago and San Francisco.

The Grand Central was opened on December 12, 1879, with Adele Leonard, May Winters, Haley and West, the Tudors, Erba Robeson, the Marietta Sisters, Minnie Coup, the LeClair Sisters and Viola Wray on stage. Many became fixtures in Leadville's spotlight over the next few years. Thomas Kemp saw the need for cleaner entertainment, so the bars were closed during the matinees. He wanted the "best people in town" to see the drama being presented. Before the construction finished, Kemp hired Billy Nuttall and Sonny Huston as managers for $1,700 per month to bring in performers from New York and Boston.

It was unusual for the manager to be accused in these robberies; however, in February 1880, Billy Nuttall was accused of stealing $1,000 from Mr. W.J. Glencross.

Mr. Glencross had taken a box at the Grand Central, and John Wall, Joseph Lowe, Billy Nuttall and a lovely waitress, Doll Lathrop, joined him. Nuttall and Glencross began talking about racehorses; Nuttall believed that his horse could beat one of the best horses in Leadville, and so the two placed a bet. Nuttall did not have the $1,000 needed for the bet, so he left the box and borrowed money from a faro dealer at the theater.

When he returned, Glencross accused him of stealing two $500 bills from his roll (he stated earlier that he had eight $500 bills). Mr. Glencross called for the police and Billy was arrested, but when the officers searched him, they found that he had no money on him. Nuttall was released due to a lack of evidence. Glencross stated that he didn't know if the bills were taken from his pocket or if they fell on the floor and were picked up by Nuttall. Charges were later dropped against Billy.

Bobby Gaylor, a local boy, got his start on this stage in 1879. His wife, May, also performed with him. In 1881, he was the lead actor of the stock company, and in November, he greeted a packed house when he portrayed Horace Tabor in the play *Prospecting*. It was a story about the start of Leadville and included portrayals of Tabor, Riche and Hook, all noted Leadville miners. When Gaylor left Leadville, he traveled east and made quite a name for himself. Never forgetting his roots, he returned to Leadville many times and played at the Tabor Opera House; a full house greeted him every time, welcoming him home.

Erba Robeson came to Leadville in December 1879 as one of the leading ladies in the original stock company at the Grand Central. She delighted the audiences with her singing and played in some of the biggest productions ever staged in Leadville, including *The Black Crook*, *Two Orphans* and *The Man from Texas*.

Erba was often mentioned in the society columns for wearing lavish diamond necklaces, brooches and rings while performing or for a night on the town. While starring in *The Black Crook*, she returned to her dressing room one night and was horrified to find that all of her jewelry had been stolen, except for the diamond piece she was wearing.

Sergeant Byrne and Officer Jessup investigated the theft, operating on the theory the only people who would have gone unnoticed backstage were those employed by the theater. Some of the jewels were found at a local pawnshop, and the clerk revealed that they had been pawned by Horace Roberts and John Doe, two actors in the *Black Crook*. The men confessed and told the officers where the rest of the jewels were hidden in Tiger Alley.

Erba often played one of the leading female parts but also met with great success playing opposite Gus Mills in role reversals—he would play a leading female part and Erba would assume the male lead. Gus returned to the Grand Central in *Pocahontas* as its "leading lady" in January 1881. and Erba played the role of John Smith; the audience was delighted and packed the house. After the success of this, he played the leading role of Morgiana in *Forty Thieves*, while Erba played the male lead of Ali Baba with the same success.

Erba left Leadville in 1882, traveling to San Francisco and New York. She returned to Leadville in 1888 as the headline act at Ben Loeb's Sporting Hall; many in Leadville remembered her and packed the house to see an old friend. On February 13, 1912, she returned to the stage of the Tabor Opera House in the cast of the *Chorus Lady*.

In a January 16, 1923 article in the *Herald Democrat*, Erba was quoted as saying, "I was a bright and popular star in Leadville in '79—the most popular woman—my photo in every house, in every store and in a sense was the idol of the public. Now there are not six persons in Leadville who ever heard my name." Never forgetting where she got her start, she always spoke fondly of her time in Leadville, saying, "How I always loved that old town; at one time I was a part of it." Erba died in 1935.

The Tudor family was employed in 1879 by the Grand Central, where they quickly became one of Leadville's favorite acts. This group consisted of John Tudor, wife Amy and their niece, Lillie Tudor. One of the disadvantages of having your family on stage every night was that everyone knew where you were and when your house was empty. On January 20, 1880, thieves broke into the Tudors' house on lower State Street and took their time going through the house, stealing every valuable they could find. Some of the items stolen included several hundred dollars, two diamond rings, a diamond cross, a gold watch, three suits, nine blue shirts, a sealskin purse, several framed sketches from England, ladies' silk dresses, silk tights, boots and shoes, along with a large amount of sheet music.

A few days later, one of the theater patrons reported that some of the missing items were at a pawnshop on Chestnut Street. Officer Allen went to the pawnshop and tracked down the thieves at the Pioneer Club. They admitted the theft, and about half of the property worth $700 was recovered. In February 1881, the Tudors left town to open the Comique Theater in Aspen.

A few years later, they returned to Leadville, and John became the stage manager for several theaters, including Ben Loeb's, Mike Goldsmith's and McDaniel's. Amy and Lillie occasionally performed at those theaters, too. On August 11, 1887, Amy Tudor died from heart problems and was laid to rest at Evergreen Cemetery. LillieTudor left Leadville and toured as a variety theater actress.

One of the largest audiences to ever attend an address was on January 9, 1880, when Charles E. Thomas addressed the theater on the famine in Ireland. It was standing room only to hear what was going on in the home country. More than $1,750 was raised to send to Ireland to help in the relief. Newspaper reports said that the wine flowed like ginger ale that night, seeing as most of the audience was Irish.

Leadville was fairly tolerant when it came to African Americans. They worked side by side in the mines and are buried next to one another at the cemetery. However, in March 1880, Billy Wilmarth, a charcoal dealer, noticed that three more "Negro" men had joined the minstrels at the Grand Central Theater. He was so angry that he raised the price of the charcoal he sold to the Grand Central for use in its stoves.

In April, Charles Howard and Ned Sullivan left their positions at the Tabor Opera House to produce *The Black Crook* at the Grand Central. The

Tabor Opera House turned down the production, saying that it was not a good fit for its theater—possibly *The Black Crook* was a little too much burlesque for it. It was a garish fable, based on the Faust legend; the play created a great deal of controversy and was almost universally condemned for its obscene decadence. Of course, there was no nudity, only chorus lines of shapely dancers draped in see-through robes, outlining what appeared to be beautiful naked bodies. In actuality, the girls wore silk tights. The show's charm included a glitzy mechanical onstage waterfall. No money was spared to make this production the best Leadville had yet seen, almost bankrupting Thomas Kemp.

In order to put on the show, the theater needed to make alterations to the stage, including adding a trapdoor. The production included mechanical walking skeletons, plaster winged dragons and gigantic monsters. Actors were frazzled by the extra practices, the cost of the wardrobe and the continued construction during rehearsals. One of the stars was another Tabor Opera House performer, Madame Morlacchi, wife of Texas Jack. She was joined by Eddie Foy; his wife, Rose Howland; T.C. Howard; and E.P. Sullivan. Kemp closed the bars and cigar rooms for a Friday matinee so ladies and children could enjoy the show.

Nothing this grand had ever played on a Leadville stage, and it would be quite a long time before this performance would be matched. Howard and Sullivan had planned to take the show on the road but decided to stay in Leadville to do more large productions. They gave another grand performance in June 1880, with the opening of *Around the World in Eighty Days*. This show rivaled *The Black Crook* and played to a sold-out crowd every night. They had "stolen" another leading star from the Tabor Opera House when Frank Roche joined the cast. *Around the World in Eighty Days* was not offered to the Tabor Opera House.

In June, Fay Templeton's troupe was on its way to Leadville to perform at the Grand Central Theater. The players arrived at Chalk Creek Ranch, and five actors got off the stage to board another Barlow and Sander's stage for Leadville. They took seats on top of the stage, but Mr. Ornauer, a tailor from Denver, was already seated. The driver refused to leave with such a large group on top and ordered Ornauer off. He refused and drew a revolver, whereupon one of the actors joking told the troupe to draw their guns. One stepped in front of Ornauer, daring him to shoot; the entire troupe laughed at this display. He finally conceded his seat and purchased a ride with a hack. Upon his arrival, he swore out warrants to have the actors arrested. Mr. Templeton, Mr. Buckley, Mr. W. Speck, Miss Camille

Valencio and Mr. Ed Duffy were all arrested and charged with breach of the peace. The charges were later dropped on all but Duffy, who was fined three dollars.

In November, Kemp again leased the theater to Billy Nuttall. He brought in James H. Love as the business manager in the hopes that the Grand Central could make a profit. The size of the theater made the cost of running it much higher than the smaller theaters, but Nuttall hoped that he could make it successful.

Soon, it was evident that he could not make things work; one of Nuttall's creditors sent the police to collect the day's receipts to pay a $500 lien. He must have gotten word they were coming because they found the cash drawers held only a few dollars.

On January 14, 1881, a most unusual event was held in the Grand Central: a wake for "Pap" Wyman. Pap was the owner of the Wyman Block and Theater and came to Leadville in 1877. He was considered one of the city's most colorful citizens, and the wake was given to honor him for his civic associations, social characteristics and local contributions. Wyman was alive and well; he even attended the night's festivities. A letter paying tribute to Wyman was read, proclaiming and thanking him for his accomplishments. He was presented with a gold-headed cane, engraved with "To C.E. Wyman, the 'Coming Man from Leadville' from his friends." Wyman was touched by the surprise wake and the sentiment from his friends; he was one of the few men to ever attend his own wake.

The night of January 27, there was a little drama going on while the actors were performing *The Enchanted Mine*. Harry Moffitt and "Little Jonnie" were watching the play from one of the boxes when Moffitt began making comments about a woman in another box. Little Johnnie got so angry he took out a revolver and began beating Moffitt over the head. Blood was streaming down Moffitt's face, and his loud cries were heard on the stage, halting the show. Luckily, Moffitt was not seriously injured, but both men were arrested. The next day, they were fined five dollars for breach of peace.

On January 30, 1881, this poem appeared in the *Leadville Daily Democrat*:

Oh where is my boy to-night.
Where is my tender youth a roaming?
A mother sang in anxious tones.
At twilights yellow gloaming.
Well that fragile youth was mile-away.

Quite comfortably fixed, you see.
With a bouncing girl of two hundred pounds.
A hovering on his knee—at the Grand Central Theatre.

All of the actors performed in a farewell performance of *Two Orphans* for Billy Nuttall on February 4, 1881. He left for Denver shortly thereafter. At the age of sixty-three, Billy committed suicide on September 22, 1896, drinking an overdose of laudanum.

Kemp then leased the Grand Central to Con Caddigan and Charlie Search, who in turn hired C.C. Lowe to manage the theater. He announced that he would run it as a legitimate theater "in apple-pie order." During the management of Search and Caddigan, the Grand Central was most successful and competed with the Tabor Opera House. When audiences grew tired of the current stock company, Search went on the road, scouting for new actors.

In the winter of 1881, they reopened the theater, employing twenty-six actors and actresses from New York. One was the LeClair family—Rose, Jim and James. Rose was a graceful and beautiful young lady who performed an act on the stage called "Leap for Life." This was an amazing gymnastic feat as Jim tossed Rose through a flaming hoop of daggers to James on the other side.

The LeClairs were known for their acting skills as well. They would go from a comedy sketch to tragedy to the trapeze, all in an hour. The diversity of this group thrilled audiences, who leaped to their feet, clapping so hard that the building shook.

The talk of the town on March 23 was the masquerade ball; everyone was dressed in elaborate costumes, and a colorful light show was presented during the dance. The fountains were illuminated by lights, and suspended from the dome was a large ball, emitting a perfume that infused the whole ballroom with a fragrance said to take the crowd "back to fairy tale times."

In April 1881, Kemp sold the theater to T.S. Schlessinger, who asked Caddigan and Search to continue managing the theater. Schlessinger purchased the Grand Central after his theater, the McDaniel's Theater, burned to the ground.

On April 28, 1881, another elaborate masquerade ball was held at the Grand Central. No one could have predicted the drama that unfolded—it was as good as any Shakespeare tragedy that played on that very stage. The theater was packed with people, all elegantly dressed in costume and with finely crafted masks. One mysterious lady caught everyone's attention; she never removed her mask or told anyone her name. Dance partner after partner tried to get her to reveal herself; one even tried to remove her mask by force. She seemed to watch one particular gentleman and then suddenly rushed out of the theater.

The next day, everyone knew the identity of the masked woman, as her story appeared in the newspaper. Kate Berry went to the theater to spy on her husband, as he had been keeping unusual hours. At the ball, she spotted him in the arms of another and left brokenhearted.

Kate returned home and took an overdose of morphine. She wrote two words on the wall for her wandering husband: "Good Bye." Mr. Berry returned home in the early morning hours of the twenty-ninth and found his wife sprawled on the bed. Unable to wake her, he sent for the doctor. Then he saw the words she left for him. With her lying in his arms, he promised that he would never stray again if she woke. The doctor arrived in time and was able to revive Kate.

The Grand Central Orchestra was conducted by Anton "Tony" Zilm and consisted of twenty-eight musicians. Matt O'Reardon, one musician, was also the composer of "The Dream of Love Is O'er" and the conductor of the Alice Oates Opera Company. He was engaged to Alice for a short time before she called off the engagement and sent him packing. O'Reardon composed the song about her and later came to Leadville, drinking his sorrows. In 1884, he died of a broken heart in Louisville, Kentucky. O'Reardon's other songs included "Gathering Shells by the Sea Shore," "Only an Ivy Leaf" and "Marriage Bells."

The theater was closed in October 1881 for extensive renovations. Patrons had complained that the theater was too cold, so a new steam heating system was added. A twenty-horsepower boiler was fitted under the stage, and another large boiler heated the entire building through 2,800 feet of steam pipe.

In the fall, Caddigan and Search gave up the lease, and Charles Lowe took over the lease and management of the theater. In February, Lowe went to Chicago, Illinois, to secure new talent, and during his absence, he placed his nephew in charge.

One evening, George Fisher, from the Bank of Leadville, came to inquire why no deposit had been made for the week's receipts. To this, the nephew replied that he had taken the money to repay a debt Lowe owed him. Without the deposit, Mr. Fisher could not pay the actors and the loan on the theater. Lowe's nephew stated that this was not his concern. Mr. Fisher assumed that Lowe had left town in order to avoid money problems, and so he closed the theater and told the staff that they could help themselves to the stock in the wine rooms in lieu of a paycheck.

The Globe Theater

Charlie Lowe returned to find his theater closed, wine rooms looted and his nephew having left town. He looked for financial assistance to reopen the theater and approached Mike Goldsmith, who bought out Lowe's lease and brought in Joe Lowe to manage the theater. Goldsmith operated a small theater on State Street, called the Globe, but it was too small for the type of acts that he wanted to present.

Goldsmith remodeled the theater, replaced the gaslights with all new electric lights and installed new carpet. The theater was repainted and thoroughly cleaned. George Heiman, a New York scene designer, was hired to paint new stage scenes. Goldsmith also hired Charles Boyd to be the stage manager because Boyd had helped make the old Globe Theater a success. On March 3, 1882, Goldsmith and Lowe reopened the theater as the Globe Theater, with the new actors and actresses Lowe secured in Chicago.

The first few months of their management, they packed the house—about three thousand people per night. During that time, it is said that wine flowed like water from the bars. The partnership was short-lived, and soon Goldsmith bought out Joe Lowe's interest.

Goldsmith was thrilled with the bookings. On May 20, 1882, he presented May Smith, leading lady in the *Little Detective*, with a token of his appreciation. During the intermission, leading man Charles Edmunds called May to the center stage and presented to her a small jeweled case containing a gold medal from Mike Goldsmith.

Unbeknownst to Goldsmith, he was about to get his own surprise. Edmunds then called Goldsmith to the stage, too. At first he was reluctant, but after the house began shouting his name, he relented. Charles Edmunds then presented him with a handsome solitaire diamond ring, stating, "This is a slight token of our esteem and we hope you will wear it, and appreciate it as symbolical of the purity of the wishes of your performers and attachés of the Globe Theater for your success." Goldsmith was stunned with the gift and the appreciation.

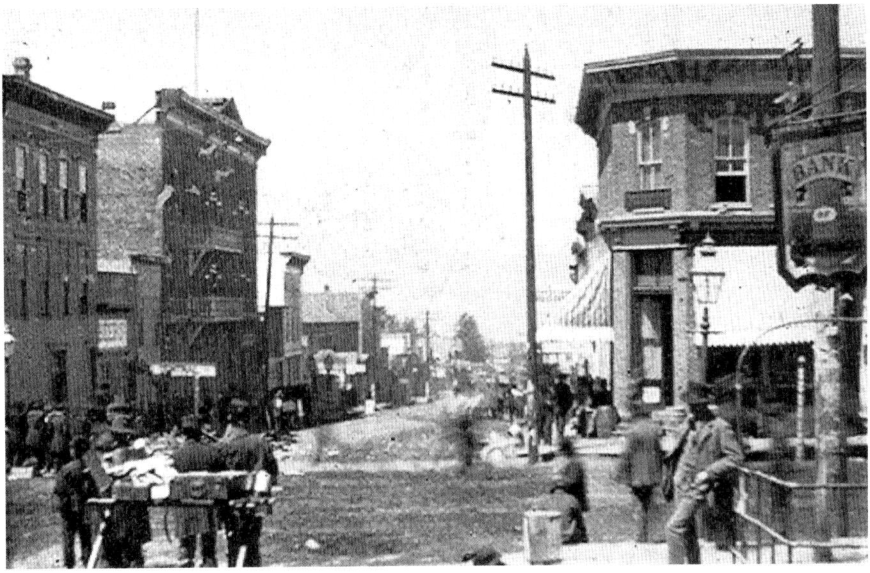

Globe Theater in about 1882. *Courtesy of the Colorado Mountain History Collection, Lake County Public Library.*

It seemed that the theater's reputation was changing. Goldsmith hired famous pianist W.F. Sheridan, who continued to help Goldsmith pack the house. He also booked Frank LaVarnie's play the *James Boys: The Missouri Outlaws*, about the famous Frank and Jesse James brothers. LaVarnie sued other playwrights to keep the exclusive rights to this tale. The performance was so popular that LaVarnie stayed for an encore two more nights, performing in *Four Aces*—this was the first time the play had been performed in Leadville.

Goldsmith experienced some of his greatest success with his theater, but tragedy struck when his daughter, Bertie, became sick with pneumonia and died a few days later. Many of the performers attended the funeral service for the eight-year-old girl. Goldsmith's children spent a great deal of time at the theater and were close to many of the actors and actresses. Frank LaVarnie even wrote a poem in honor of the girl:

> *Little Bertie Goldsmith*
> *God bless our darling*
> *She's left this world for rest: Her sweet smiles we'll ne'er see again*

Bertie with god is best
Her resting place we'll cherish
Our Saviour'll ne'er forget
To welcome back to outstretched arms
Our child who's living yet
Like all who have departed
We'll miss her from our happy home: Was none but her' alone,
And now that she's beneath the god
God bless her evermore
Twill break our hearts (though she with god)
To miss her from shore.
Oh Papa dear, I'm wandering off
To some strange land away: To me while I delay
And when I'm with the angels,
I hope you'll always try
To think of 'Little Bertie,"
Who will never die.
June 7, 1882

In October 1882, Mike Goldsmith hoped to improve the image of the Globe Theater by booking a mass meeting of the Republicans of Leadville. The keynote speaker was John Burns Belford, a member of the Colorado Supreme Court. Not all the regular patrons got the message that the normal nightly entertainment had been canceled. One of the boxes got out of hand, calling for the waitress to bring more drinks and yelling drunken slurs at the stage—once again proving that this theater would never rise above the standing of a burlesque theater.

Foster's Zoo Theater

Goldsmith turned the management of the Globe over to Ned Forester and Pap Wyman in February 1883. The name changed again, to Foster's Zoo. In April, they bought Goldsmith out for $1,000.

The Zoo was known for its racy entertainment, boxing and wrestling matches but was not known as a legitimate theater. The bars served watered-down liquor late into the night by the prettiest waitresses. Everything changed on April 7 when Foster brought *The Black Crook* back for the fifth time. The production was brought from New York by Charlie Howard, who had staged the very first production a few years earlier.

The theater closed the bars and gave the waitresses the night off. Boxes sold for $7.50 on the third floor and $5.00 on the second floor. Each box was designed to seat five people, and $1.00 was added for those wishing to have additional people; second floor seats sold for $0.50 or $0.75 each. There was such a demand for tickets that they were resold on the street for $5.00 to $7.00 each. No matter what seat they had, or how much they paid, it was hailed as the best show ever held in Leadville. The costumes were magnificent, the special effects outstanding and the ballet splendid.

It was the largest crowd Foster ever had, and he took steps to turn the theater back into a legitimate theater. He was rewarded with full houses for *Young Mrs. Winthrop* and *The Gold Hunters of the Black Hills*. Foster's decision to change the focus of the theater could not have come at a better time.

William Bush was managing the Tabor Grand Opera House in Denver and decided that any performance booked at a competitive theater in Leadville, rather than the Tabor Opera House, would not be permitted to book at the Tabor Grand Opera House in Denver. This left very good companies looking for a place to play in Leadville. Foster stepped up to meet this need and was handsomely rewarded; the decision did, however, hurt the Tabor Opera House.

It also brought two old rivals, Mike Goldsmith and Ned Foster, together to run the Zoo and the National Theater under joint management. The National Theater booked variety acts, boxing and wrestling matches—entertainment geared toward male patrons. There was no charge for admission; the money was made off sales from the bar. The Zoo Theater was a legitimate theater, booking the best traveling shows and charging admission.

In the spring of 1883, rumors began to fly that someone was going to burn down the Zoo Theater. Foster warned his employees to be extra vigilant; he had reason to fear, since other theaters had been burned down by arsonists. On June 19, two waitresses came to the property man and reported that they had seen someone lurking around the prop room. The property man immediately checked and saw two figures on the floor; surely they were there to rob the theater. He ran to tell Foster, who excitedly grabbed his gun and ran down the street to his theater. In his rush, he tripped and fell down the stairs, injuring his leg, but he continued to where the culprits were. By the sliver of light coming in from a window, he saw the two figures on the floor and drew his gun, firing three shots at the men. Seeing no movement, a lamp was lit, only to discover that the figures were nothing more than two dummies someone had laid on the floor. A few days afterward, Foster was able to laugh about the incident, even though he still bore the bruises from his fall.

A theater group should always know its audience. This was a hard lesson learned by the Earle Company on December 12, 1883. The troupe performed *The Black Diamond*, a play about the coal mining districts of Pennsylvania, with one act portraying a group of masked men known as the Molly Maguires. The troupe failed to realize that Leadville housed a large group of Molly Maguires, some hiding from the law themselves. As the troupe portrayed the scene, a large group of men stood up and began throwing stones, eggs and other articles, yelling for the performers to get off the stage. The play was forced to stop, and the performers retreated to their dressing rooms. Police chased down some of the men involved, but none was convicted.

Years earlier, a play entitled *The Molly Maguires* had played at the Grand Central Theater, starring Bobby Gaylor and Laura LeClair; however, the play was empathic to their cause and portrayed them in a positive light. Also, LeClair and Gaylor were both Leadville actors. These might be the reasons why their play was greeted by eager audiences every night and why the Earle Company was accosted.

Although Foster packed the house with theatrical performances, boxing was becoming more popular, and it was soon added to the venue at the Zoo. Patrons paid twice as much for a seat to watch a good fight. The house made a killing from the bars, plus a percentage off any bets placed.

In July 1883, Foster booked Charles Mitchell, the "Bloody Englishman," and offered any man $100 who could stay in the ring for four three-minute rounds. The July 7 bout was announced as Charlie Mitchell versus James Clark of Leadville. Before the fight, Dennis Hayes, a forty-five-year-old bartender, challenged Mitchell. He said that the fight had been fixed—if not, then surely Mitchell would have no problem fighting him. Foster agreed, adding $50 to the pot if Hayes could stay four rounds.

Mitchell pounded on Hayes mercilessly in the second round, bloodying his nose and knocking him down several times. Even so, Hayes managed to last the four rounds. When it was over, Mitchell sulked off, and the crowd rushed the stage to shake the hand of the man who stood against the "Bloody Englishman." The next night, Mitchell took on Clark, knocking him out in the second round. To some, this confirmed what Hayes had said about the fight being fixed; others were just in awe of Hayes.

The third night of Mitchell's visit was the most disappointing. He was matched against William Lynn, Colorado's middleweight champion, and he crushed Lynn in the first round. When the bell rang for the second round, Lynn stayed in his corner; the crowd went wild. Mitchell engaged him in the corner; Lynn hung on to the rope, even dodging under the ropes. Mitchell became so angry that he threw his gloves to the floor and left the ring, refusing to return. More than two thousand people paid to see a good fight, and they were disappointed with Lynn's cowardly performance. Twenty-five dollars was raised to buy Lynn a train ticket out of town.

On December 29, 1883, police were forced to put an end to a fight at the Zoo. John L. Sullivan, the world heavyweight boxing champion, fought Pete McCourt, middleweight champion. Before the fight, Sullivan took a tour of Leadville and the surrounding area. While on the tour, he and his party began drinking heavily; by the time Sullivan stepped into the ring, he was quite drunk. Instead of a fight, a brawl occurred. McCourt hit Sullivan over the head with a chair, and in retaliation, Sullivan threw an oil lamp. Luckily the wick went out as the lamp was thrown, although the thought of fire still caused the crowd to rush out of the building.

Marshal Ed Cudihee rushed in to put an end to the brawl, but while placing Sullivan under arrest, Sullivan resisted. The officer drew his revolver and said, "If you come near me, I will put a bullet through you," whereupon Sullivan backed off. Cudihee allowed Sullivan's friends to take him back to his hotel to sleep it off. The next night, Sullivan was scheduled to appear again; however, he sent word that he was on his deathbed with a hemorrhage. The following day, he had recovered enough to take the train out of Leadville.

The Cricket Theater

In February 1884, the theater was leased to Gus Harris and Ike Morris and renamed the Cricket Theater. It was renovated and updated scenes were painted and installed. It was turned over to a stock company that offered a variety of nightly entertainment, including a trapeze artist and horizontal bar entertainment. The theater boasted that it had the prettiest waitresses in Leadville, thus appealing to the gentlemen patrons. This was a short-lived venture, and on March 18, the theater closed its doors, leaving the stage dark at last.

In May, the Bank of Leadville foreclosed on the theater. It was leased to Ben Dixon and Ed Cudihee. Dixon began renovations with the intentions of running it as a vaudeville theater.

At one o'clock in the morning on June 18, the cry of "Fire!" was heard. People rushed from the bars, cribs and apartments to see flames shooting out of the building. It was empty for its grand reopening on June 20. Firemen quickly arrived on scene and rushed into the building but were forced out by the thick black smoke.

The firemen reported that the bulk of the fire was on the stage, engulfing the painted drops and scenes. Soon they decided that there was no way to save the theater, but they needed to collapse it as soon as possible to save the Liberty Hall and the Little Casino Saloon on either side.

Two firemen, Charles Sawyer and J.H. Mallory, and D.C. McCune, a volunteer, rushed inside in order to cut the great columns that held up the roof. Once inside, the roof and part of the wall caved in, trapping them in the rubble. Outside, they could hear their screams for help. A black man named "Shorty" McCloud, in a gallant effort, managed to hoist a piece of the wall up, freeing Charles Sawyer.

Additional rescue attempts were made by cutting a hole in the wall of the Liberty Hall in order to enter the burning building. This caused the fire to enter the Liberty Hall and forced the firefighters back to the street. From there, they could only watch as the walls caved in completely. Hooks were attached to the front of the Liberty Hall, and it was also pulled down in the hopes of stopping the destructive blaze. Screams from J.H. Mallory were heard as he pleaded, "If you can't get me out then just shoot me." The following day, the remains of Mallory and McCune were recovered.

An inquest was held to determine the cause of the fire and the death of the two men. Mike Goldsmith, owner of the Liberty Hall, testified that he rushed to the scene and saw clouds of thick black smoke but detected no smell of coal oil or benzene. He also said that there was a large pile of rubble in the building and that some worker could have carelessly thrown a cigar in the pile, causing it to smolder and light the fire.

Ben Dixon testified that the theater was closed and that no one was sleeping there, but someone could have gotten in the back, where there were a few broken windows. City Alderman C.C. Joy testified that he heard the calls of "Fire!" from his rooms on Harrison Avenue, rushed outside and saw that the doors of the theater were open. He did notice a strong smell of coal oil in the air—the same smell he experienced a few years earlier at the Coliseum fire. The inquest found that the cause of the fire was arson.

Four buildings—the Grand Central, the Liberty Hall (Bon Ton Dance Hall), the Little Casino and the Eureka Restaurant—were lost that day.

In February 1886, a gentleman from Ireland asked for permission to excavate the ruins of the Grand Central. He was looking for the entrance to a tunnel that ran from the Comique Theater to the Grand Central, under State and Chestnut Streets. It had been used as a transport system for a grocer's warehouse on Chestnut Street, and later to connect the Tontine Restaurant at 140 Chestnut to the Comique Theater.

The gentleman's brother was last seen at the Tontine before he disappeared. Other men had disappeared from the Tontine, and this gentleman believed that their bodies, as well as well as his brother's, might be in the tunnel. If he was successful, it has been lost in time, as no documentation has been found on their identities or the results of the search.

New Athenaeum Theater

Located at 120 West State Street, this two-story frame building was erected in 1878 by Hiram P. Marston as a burlesque theater. In August 1879, Mabel River reopened the theater as the New Athenaeum. One of the most notable features was how the fire barrels on the roof gave the allure of floating fire. Mabel hung banners up and down State Street to promote her great theater, but she was unable to compete with the larger theaters in town. That same month, she packed her bags and belongings and left in the middle of the night.

It was reopened by the Howard & Laiscell Company. "Tableaux" is French for "living picture," and this theater was known for its "leg shows" or tableaux. The term describes a striking group of suitably costumed actresses, carefully posed, who do not speak or move throughout the play. One of the most popular was *Carbonate Mines*, where the lady performers were dressed as representations of Leadville mines: the Little Chief, the Robert E. Lee, the Highland Mary, the Wolfetone and the Maid of Erin.

Shortly after opening under new management, Charlie Howard took a job as front of the house manager at the Tabor Opera House. After Howard left, the theater could not compete with the Olympic or the Coliseum, and the doors closed.

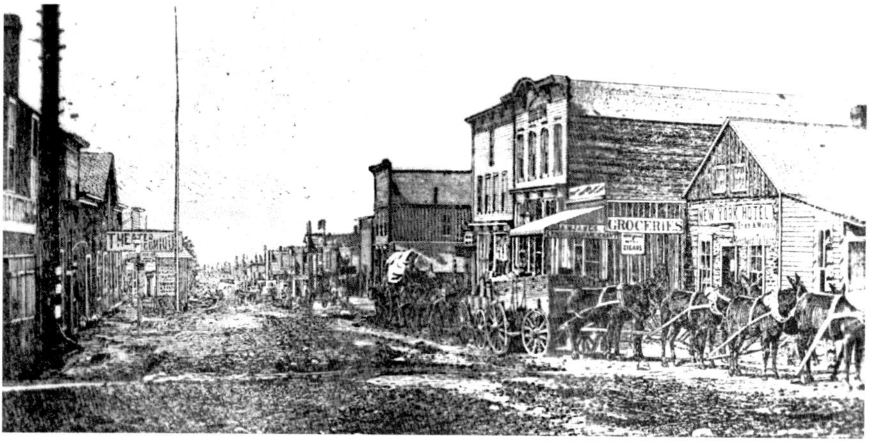

State Street postcard.

New Leadville Theater

In the spring of 1880, the theater was sold to James McDaniel and Gus Vogus, who renamed it the New Leadville Theater, or McDaniel's Theater. It was not your traditional Shakespeare theater. McDaniel's theaters were known for their scantily dressed women, excessive liquor and seedy entertainment. To draw people in, he stationed a band run by the Schlessinger brothers outside on the street.

For this type of entertainment, McDaniel was handsomely rewarded as the money flowed in. McDaniel was a well-known, traveling variety theater man who also had a solid reputation in Cheyenne and Dodge City.

One day, a lustful suitor wooed Jennie "Mollie" Mickie away from her home in Illinois when she was just a young girl. He abandoned her in Cheyenne, Wyoming, and she had no choice but to take a job as a vaudeville actress with James McDaniel's troupe.

In May 1876, while traveling with the troupe in the Dakotas, she met and fell in love with Jim May. It is reported that Mollie also caught the eye of Jim's brother, "Boone" May. One night, a fight broke out in the Gem Theater, and Boone grabbed a gun with the intent of shooting his brother but shot Mollie instead. Luckily, the bullet was deflected by the boning in her corset.

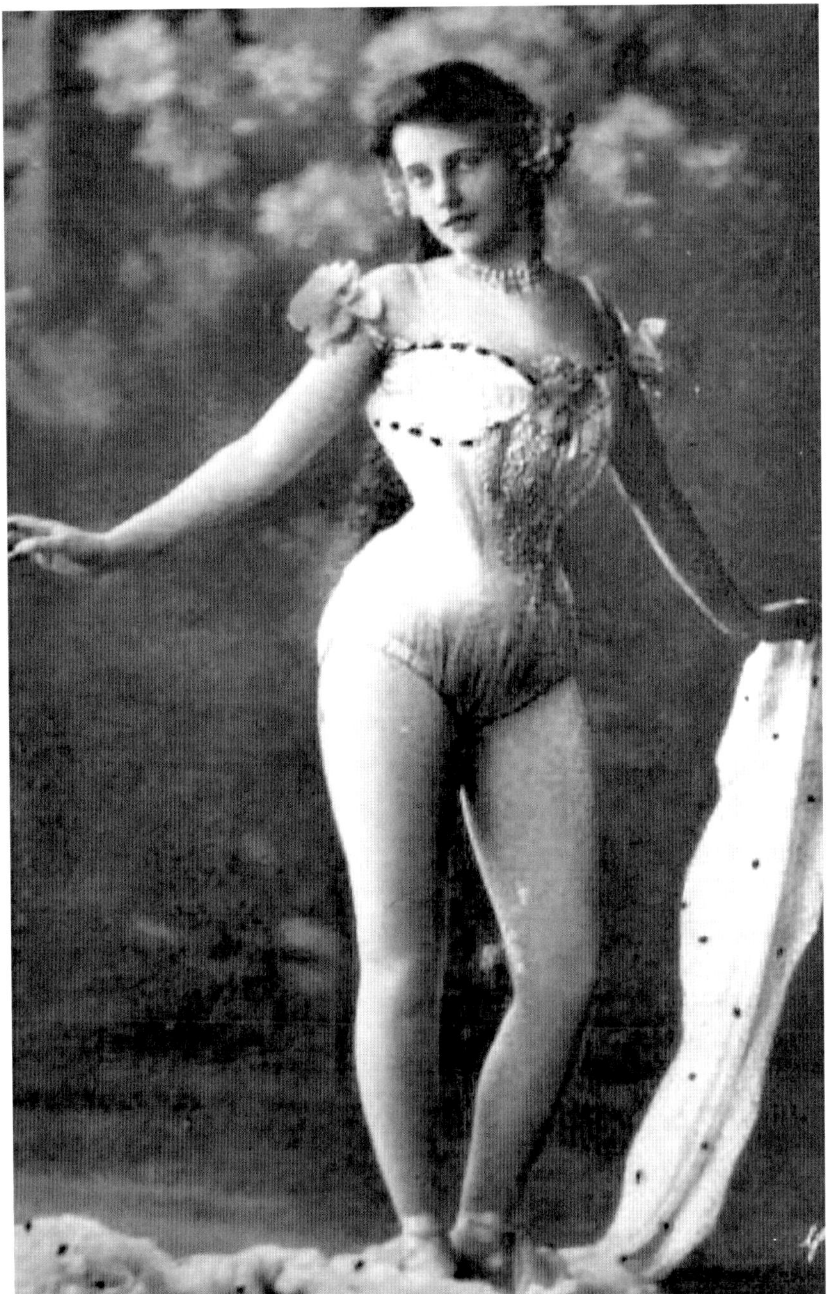

Burlesque dancer, circa 1880.

After this incident, Jim no longer wanted to marry Mollie, but she took his last name as her own. Mollie was not single for long; she set her sights on Jim Brown, a local banjo player. The relationship was short-lived, for it seems that Jim was already taken. When Fanny Garretson, the bride-to-be, got word of the relationship, she confronted Mollie while they were riding in a carriage; a fight broke out, and Fanny bit off part of Mollie's ear.

Mollie left the troupe, headed to Leadville and opened a bordello and dance hall, the Bon Ton, on West Fifth Street. She became Leadville's most famous madam. Mollie May died in Leadville on April 10, 1887, at thirty-eight years old.

In February 1881, McDaniel sold two-thirds of the theater to the Schlessinger brothers and one-third to Mr. Isendraft, a silent partner. McDaniel left Leadville and toured the United States with his troupe. The theater was repainted; boxes were added to the upstairs balcony, with lace curtains in each box; backdrop curtains were painted for the stage; and the theater was reopened with a larger stock company.

March 29, 1881, was a rather routine evening at the theater until 11:00 p.m. T.S. Schlessinger was in an upstairs room when he heard crackling sounds. He went to the window and noticed flames leaping out of the Pioneer Club next door. People ran out of several buildings to see the fire take hold of the Pioneer. Schlessinger and volunteers rushed into the theater to save what they could and threw everything into the middle of the street.

Fire crews arrived and put streams of water on the Pioneer Club and the theater; the fire spread quickly, taking an aggressive hold and reaching the Capital Restaurant. Sure that the fire would take the whole block, Chief Fonda made a decision to evacuate the rest of the street. There were four streams of water on the burning buildings, but they were not able to get it under control. Sparks flew, landing on the roofs of the tenements in Tiger Alley, behind the burning buildings.

Chief Fonda removed the water directed at the burning buildings and used it to soak the rest of the block. His decision saved the rest of the block. Schlessinger could only watch as the fire destroyed the theater, leaving a pile of ashes.

The Gaiety Theater

Mabel River was the first owner of the Gaiety Theater, at 127 State Street. She opened in July 1879, and Mabel herself was the top attraction. The Gaiety was a variety theater, known to have many acts per day, including trick dogs, gymnasts and tightrope walkers, as well as plays. River was unable to compete with the larger theaters though.

In January 1881, Lottie May was the first female manager of the day-to-day operations of a theater in Leadville. She stayed for a few short months before leaving Leadville, but her management paved the way for other women to be successful managers.

One of the biggest crowd pleasers was E.J. Hoyt, aka "Buckskin Joe" Hoyt. He performed a variety of tumbling, trapeze and tightrope walking acts. One of his most dramatic acts happened outside. Buckskin Joe stretched a tightrope across State Street and pushed a wheelbarrow across the tightrope. In the middle, Belle Laiscell passed him. Another time, when they were doing the same act with the rope between the buildings, Hoyt did not have the wheelbarrow. Instead, he swung under the rope in the middle and hung there as she passed. He then swung himself back up and went the rest of the way. The crowd went wild.

During his time at the Gaiety Theater, Hoyt made twenty-eight walks inside, and every night was different. He walked with a hoop or blindfolded, and even once he went with a bag over his head.

Hoyt said that during his time at the Gaiety, he ran into Frank and Jesse James. The James brothers reserved a box to see him perform. E.J. made

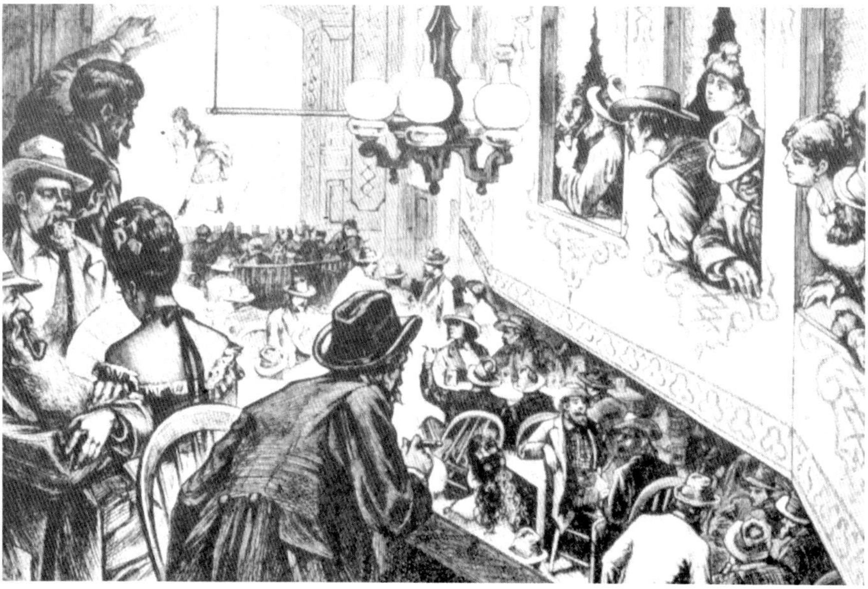

Depiction of the interior of the Gaiety Theater 1879. *Courtesy of the Colorado Mountain History Collection, Lake County Public Library.*

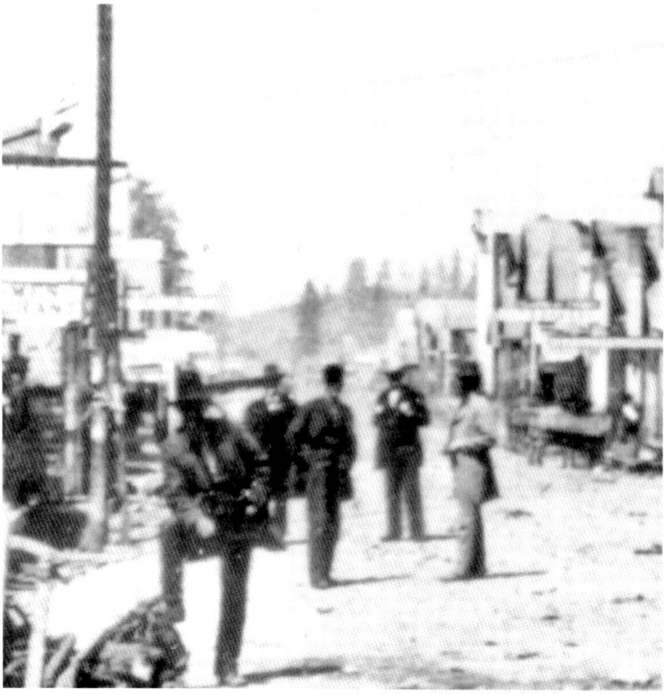

State Street in 1881 showing the tightrope stretched between the Gaiety Theater and the New Leadville Theater. *Courtesy of the Colorado Mountain History Collection, Lake County Public Library.*

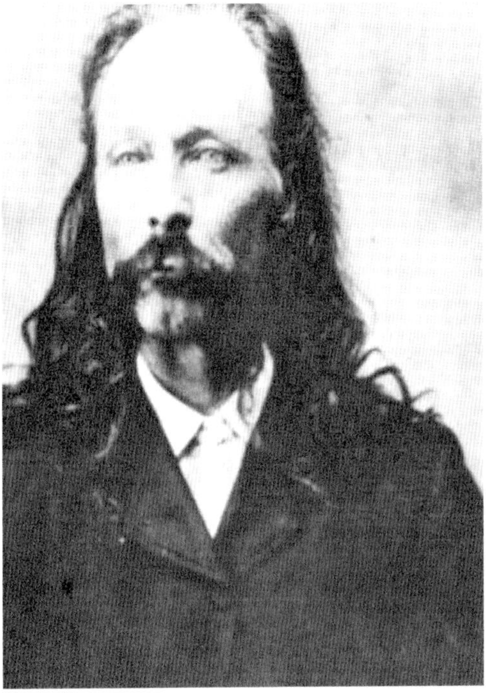

E.J. Hoyt ("Buckskin Joe") before cutting his hair and mustache.

sure that they were well cared for during the evening's entertainment; he even arranged for a private waiter. He remarked that the James brothers were good customers and dropped about $200.00 dollars in tips, $0.25 cigars and $7.00 bottles of wine. Although the James brothers were known to have a mining claim at Soda Springs, just outside Leadville, we only have Hoyt's word that this actually happened.

Hoyt used some of the money he made at the Gaiety to invest in Leadville's mining claims. In the summer of 1880, Hoyt vowed that he would not cut his hair until he was worth $50,000. By 1884, his mining investments paid off. His hair measured fifteen inches and his mustache six inches. Then he cut both. Hoyt left Leadville for other adventures, returning occasionally to check on his mining interests.

New Central Theater

Laura LeClair and her sister, Maggie, arrived in Leadville in December 1879. They debuted at the opening night of the Grand Central Theater. Laura worked for several different theaters until she opened the New Central Theater at 116 West State Street.

James McDaniel and Laura LeClair formed a partnership, but unfortunately it ended before the opening on June 7, 1886. Laura became the sole owner and hired her brother, James, to manage the theater while she performed in many of the productions. Later, she assumed the management as well.

In 1887, Susie Stokes and Annie Pertie left the theater and went to work for Mike Goldsmith's theater. LeClair was angry that Goldsmith had stolen her actresses and sued all three for breach of contract. The judge sided with LeClair, and the girls were not allowed to work for the next three weeks, until their contract was completed with LeClair.

Laura was a kindhearted woman and always helped out when she could. In 1887, a man nicknamed "Dutch" came by and asked for food. Laura gave him money to go to a restaurant up the street. This scene was repeated every day, and soon Laura was paying Dutch to sweep and help out with other odd jobs. When friends asked if Laura wanted to join them for the day, she gladly accepted, leaving Dutch in charge. Upon returning, she quickly realized that her money, dresses and jewelry were gone. Dutch was nowhere to be found. Sadly, Laura filled out a warrant for his arrest, but he had left town. After that, Laura was a little less trusting.

Harry and Ida LaVeer worked as trapeze artists for several theaters between 1885 and 1886, including LeClair's, Goldsmith's and Ben Loeb's. One day, a young dance hall girl offered herself to Harry; he refused, stating that he loved his wife dearly. This angered the woman, so she told Ida that Harry was seeing another woman and planning to leave her. Ida was brokenhearted and took an overdose of laudanum. Her friends found her unconscious and called for the doctor, who managed to revive her. Ida related the story the woman had told her. Although the doctor declared her out of danger, she died the next day.

Harry was inconsolable. His friends tried to help, encouraging him to return to the stage. In time, Harry did return to the stage, but one night at Loeb's, he slipped and fell off the trapeze. Harry took to his bed for several weeks, and Lottie Miranda, a fellow trapeze artist, stayed by his side and nursed him back to health.

After Harry recovered, he heard rumors why his wife had tried to take her life and blamed himself. Friends encouraged him to move on with his life, so he did. Three months after Ida's death, he married Lottie. This only caused him more grief, and two days after the wedding, Harry took his own life. His request to be buried next to Ida, his true love, was honored, and they rest at Evergreen Cemetery.

Mike Whalen, a singer at Ben Loeb's, wrote this song to memorialize his friend:

The silver moon was shining upon our little town.
The stars shone on the dying and the brave.
On the bed lay, one who had just passed away.
To be buried in a suicide's grave.
When his friends gathered round; t'was a note was found.
Saying that he was tired of life.
He was going to his rest he thought it was best.
For he could not live without his darling wife.

Chorus
The husband and the bride are sleeping side by side.
They've gone to One who judges all the brave.
They're together hand and heart, and they never more will part.
For they're lying in a suicide's grave.
The doctors they then came, but their efforts were in vain;
They did all in their power to save his life.

He made his earthly play, and his soul had passed away.
To that land where there is no care or strife.
Just three months ago to-day his wife, Ida passed away.
And it nearly broke poor little Harry's heart.
For the one he truly loved had gone to her home above.
Now they're together, never more to part.
When the subscription went around his friend were to be found:
They added to the list their little mite;
And this true friend Charlie Young to his dead friend he still clung.
Till in Evergreen they placed him out of site.

When Whalen performed this song on the stage, Harry's friends would gather to remember their friend. It was a touching tribute. Harry's real name was John M. Seaman; however, like so many other fallen actors, he is buried under his stage name.

In the spring of 1887, a reporter asked LeClair about business, and she replied, "Business doesn't compare with the days when desirable boxes sold at a premium and the patrons ran a race to determine who could spend the most money. In those days the patrons bought wine for the girls. Now beer is good enough and there's a limit to that."

The Leadville City Council revoked the license of the New Central Theater on September 9, 1887, in an attempt to shut it down. The council believed that the games were rigged, favoring the house. The members debated whether it was right to single out one establishment; many advocated closing all gaming houses on State Street. Finally, they voted to take no action, and the license was restored to the New Central Theater.

It is said that you cannot die of a broken heart, but tell that to John England. He visited LeClair's everyday for two years just to be near his love, Maud Whalen. On November 11, 1887, John borrowed money from his friends, purchased a ring and got the courage to ask Maud to be his wife. When he gave Maud his ring and confessed his love, the heartless soul laughed in his face. John was so upset that he left the theater, telling her that he was going to commit suicide. The next morning, his body was found in the alley behind the theater. Everyone assumed that John had committed suicide until the autopsy showed that he had died of an enlarged heart; poor John's heart was broken by love.

In the summer of 1888, Laura LeClair contracted Brisbois Photography Studio to take pictures of her theater and waitresses—with and without their tights. After Alfred Brisbois completed the work, LeClair refused to pay him.

Brisbois went to Denver and filed suit; the court found in favor of Brisbois, and LeClair was forced to pay $100 for the photos and court costs.

LeClair was not one to go away easily. She went back to court and asked for the judgment to be set aside, claiming that the photos were taken improperly—some of the girls were without their tights. The court did not see it her way and again ordered a judgment in favor of Brisbois.

That winter, Laura sold the theater to Mike Goldsmith, moved to Denver and opened the Central Theater, managing and performing there until her death in August 1889. She was considered the oldest female variety performer working in Colorado at thirty-five years old.

The Novelty Theater

A year later, Goldsmith sold the theater to Ben Loeb, changing the name to the Novelty Theater. A few months later, Loeb also purchased the Carbonate Theater from Mike Goldsmith. He cut costs by running both under the same management company. He advertised the Novelty Theater as a "palace of pleasure." Boxes cost three, five and seven dollars, depending on the size; boxes could hold two, three or five people.

Loeb's Novelty Theater was known for its loose women, rivers of alcohol, cheating tables and bar fights. Early one morning, a fight occurred between two railroad men, John Holland and L.L. Woods. Woods entered the bar and began calling Holland names, and a fight broke out. Woods had been fired from the Colorado Midland Railroad, and Holland had taken his job. Loeb ran to the door and blew his police whistle; his call for help went unanswered. He returned to the saloon and managed to get the two men apart. When doctors examined Wood's injuries, they found that most of his ear, a piece of his chin and part of his nose had been bitten off. Both men were charged for fighting in public.

On May 1, 1892, C.W. Adams was at a table in the bar when he heard a strange sound of wood creaking. He opened the door to the theater and noticed that the stage and curtains were engulfed in flames. He shouted to the three men practicing on the trapeze and told them to leave. Smoke filled the theater, and the men were having trouble seeing the ropes to get down. They jumped to the floor and managed to escape from the building with only slight injuries.

It was a windy night, and the flames quickly spread to the nearby Pioneer Club, then owned by Mike Goldsmith. Soon, the fire spread to the Red Light Dance Hall, the White House Saloon, the Mint Saloon and six cribs in the alley, owned by Nellie Shields, along with two brothels and a barbershop. By the next morning, nothing was left but ashes. Saved from the theater was Queene, Loeb's terrier, which had also been saved from two other fires in her lifetime: the Schloss Beer Hall fire and the Delmonico Concert Hall fire (and they say only cats have nine lives). Three other dogs perished in the fire.

The great destruction on State Street was blamed on the lack of water pressure from the hydrants. Calls were made to the water department asking for more water, but it took twenty minutes to get more pressure. By that time, many buildings were entirely engulfed. Loeb believed that the fire started from a candle in the dressing room of the trapeze artist. The candle was placed under a shelf and lit the shelf on fire, later igniting the costumes in the room and spreading to the stage.

The Avenue

This burlesque theater located at 116 Harrison Avenue was operated as the Rocky Mountain Theater for a few years before Ben Loeb purchased it in 1886, changing the name to the Avenue Theater. The variety theaters were always in competition with one another. In 1886, the big three were the Carbonate, the Avenue and the New Central, each trying to book the best shows and hire the prettiest girls. Loeb often sent his performers and musicians strolling down Harrison Avenue to attract customers. Occasionally, Loeb's band would be on one end of the street and Laura LeClair's on the other, trying to outdo each other.

Competition among the variety theaters was brutal, each vying for its share. Loeb promoted his theater with street parades. The *Herald Democrat* described one: "The parade was headed by a brass band of thirty pieces, followed by the broad-sword performers on horseback. After that were three black-face characters, followed by a clown and baboon act. At the end were five open carriages, filled with ladies who performed or served at the theater."

Another advertising technique was to run ads in the local newspapers, each claiming to have the prettiest waitresses in the shortest dresses. Loeb referred to his girls as "Sweet Forget-Me-Nots." They were paid fourteen dollars per week plus 10 percent of any sales they made. Many girls made their way here from the East, having read one of his advertisements for help in their local paper. When the girls arrived, they were in debt to Loeb for travel expenses, in addition to room and board for one of the rooms above

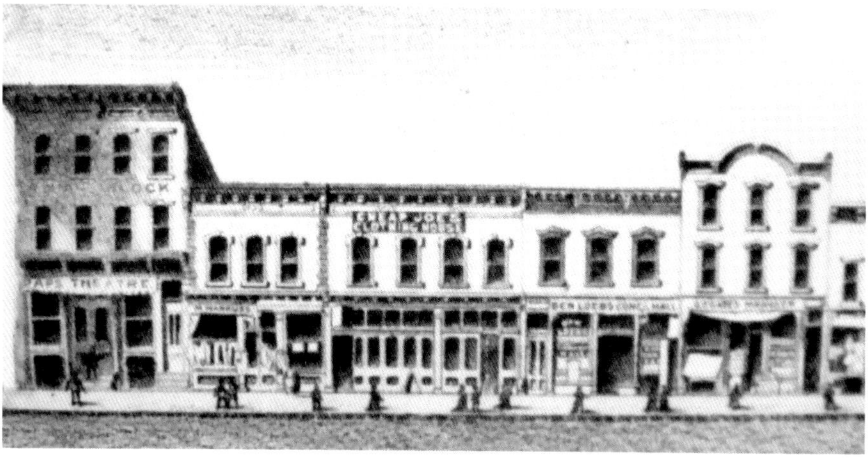

Depiction of Pap Wyman's and Ben Loeb's theater buildings. *Courtesy of the Colorado Mountain History Collection, Lake County Public Library.*

the theater. If a young lady left his employment before paying off the debt, Loeb had her arrested for grand larceny.

On August 28, 1886, the theater was bursting at the seams to see a fight between John B. Clow, Colorado's champion prizefighter, and "Omaha" Jack Davis, a local miner. Ticket sales were exceptional because people wanted to get a look at Clow's manager, the famous Bat Masterson. Masterson put up $1,000 to the winner. Many had side bets on the fight, although Clow was felt to be the favorite. The fight started out slow, with each fighter trading punches, but in the fourth round, Davis threw a few fast punches, knocking Clow out.

In October 1887, as a promotion, Loeb secured a permit from the city to have a fireworks display and bonfire outside his theater. He also advertised the twenty-five-cent admission, including a drink, a cigar and six hours of continuous entertainment.

Also in 1888, Ben Loeb ran a notice in the papers announcing that he had purchased both the Avenue and the New Central Theaters. To promote the new management, he had Mon Hewletter, a French tightrope walker, perform a free slack-wire performance from the top of his theater, across State Street.

Loeb knocked heads with the law several times during his long career in Leadville. In April 1888, Marshal White told him that he could no longer employ children to perform on stage or to run errands. Two young daughters of A.L. Bower played the violin and clarinet, while several young boys ran errands and helped as stagehands. The city council decided that a variety hall on State Street was no place for children; he was still allowed to use the boys as sign holders to advertise on Harrison Avenue, though.

In May 1889, Marshal White went into the beer halls, dance halls and theaters, stating that the city had an ordinance forbidding women from serving alcohol. He demanded that the managers stop or he would shut them down. One problem with the ordinance was Marshal White's interpretation.

Outraged, Ben Loeb went to the city and demanded that his women not be grouped under the same law as a beer or dance hall; the council needed to make the ordinance clearer. The motion passed seven to five that women could work in variety theaters and beer and dance halls but had to pay a fee of five dollars per month or they would be arrested and fined five dollars. This is the same fee system that was charged to the prostitutes; the city and society thought of these girls as one and the same.

George "the Fighting Marine" La Blanche, the famous pugilist, was hired by Loeb in 1889. He was a Canadian boxer who had quite a reputation in the East; he had only been defeated once, by Jack Dempsey. He and his manager, Charles Gleason, traveled across the United States, fighting in variety theaters.

On March 11, a large crowd gathered to see the fight between Murdy Buchanan and La Blanche. Marshal White and several deputies crowded into the theater to keep the peace; their presence allowed them a free seat. An eighteen-foot-square ring was set up at center stage, with seats surrounding. At 12:55 a.m., the fighters took the stage, and the crowd noticed that they were unevenly matched. La Blanche was five-foot-eight, 155 pounds; Buchanan was five-foot-eleven, 190 pounds. Pete Dempsey was the referee.

The fight began with Buchanan landing a hard right to La Blanche's neck, followed by an exchange of blows. Murdy was the crowd's favorite, with cheers of "Go for Murdy" and "Bully for you, Murdy." The cheering distracted Murdy, and La Blanche managed to land several good punches to Murdy's neck. Luckily, time was called, and Murdy went to his corner looking dazed.

In the second round, Murdy came out swinging, but his blows were all avoided. La Blanche countered and gave a hard left to Murdy's neck, sending him staggering across the ring. La Blanche backed away, but Murdy could not rise and so he threw in the sponge. The total fight time was three minutes and fifty-five seconds. After the fight, Loeb paid Buchanan ten dollars for his pain and expenses.

On August 28, 1890, a tragic accident occurred at the theater while Minnie Pierce was performing on the small trapeze. Her hand cramped as she was going into the turn of a hand twist, and not able to hold on to the bar, she fell ten feet to the floor, landing on her back. Stagehands carried her to her dressing room below the stage. Dr. Law was called, and although the injury was not life-threatening, she was in considerable pain.

Loeb ran a dance hall, the Palace of Pleasure, at 122 West State Street, as well as a saloon at 120 West State Street. In 1897, Leadville enacted an ordinance prohibiting the sale of liquor where women were employed. Loeb countered by serving his thirsty customers a tall glass of frothy buttermilk when they stepped up to the bar. He said, "I am running my dance hall on moral principles. State Street is no longer the wickedest place on earth, but Buttermilk Avenue."

Shortly before Ben Loeb died, the buildings were closed and stood vacant, a ghostly reminder of the past. Loeb was seventy-two years old when he died on January 21, 1912. He is buried at Evergreen Cemetery. His funeral was attended by only three people, a sad tribute to one of the last great showmen of Leadville.

Wyman's Theater

C.E. "Pap" Wyman was a colorful character in early Leadville. He built his cabin in 1878, and it was surrounded by sagebrush, but by early 1879, the sagebrush was gone, and Harrison Avenue had sprouted up around the cabin. Pap ran a small gambling operation out of the cabin and sold tickets for the Colorado lottery, consisting of thirteen winning numbers. He advertised the lottery as a weekly drawing for $15,000, as well as daily prizes.

Traffic had to go on either side of the cabin, and city officials decided that it must be torn down. Wyman became angry and surrounded the cabin with armed guards. The city offered $6,000 for land for which he had paid $200 a year earlier. Initially he refused the money, but he later gave in, and the cabin was torn down.

Using the money, he built the Wyman Block on the southeast corner of Harrison Avenue and Second Street; a three-story, wood-frame building with apartments on the second floor. The ground floor was rented to the *Leadville Herald* newspaper, and it put out the first issue at this location. When it moved to a new location, Wyman opened a saloon and theater.

Pap spent his early years as a preacher and hung a clock over the door with "Please don't swear" painted on the face. Below the clock was a Bible for those who did not heed the sign. Pap made patrons read from it to atone for their sins. It was said that thousands read from that Bible.

He refused to allow married men, especially fathers, to gamble, and he sent them home early to their wives. He didn't want them to spend their entire paycheck on drink. Drunks were not served. Pap kept a watchful eye

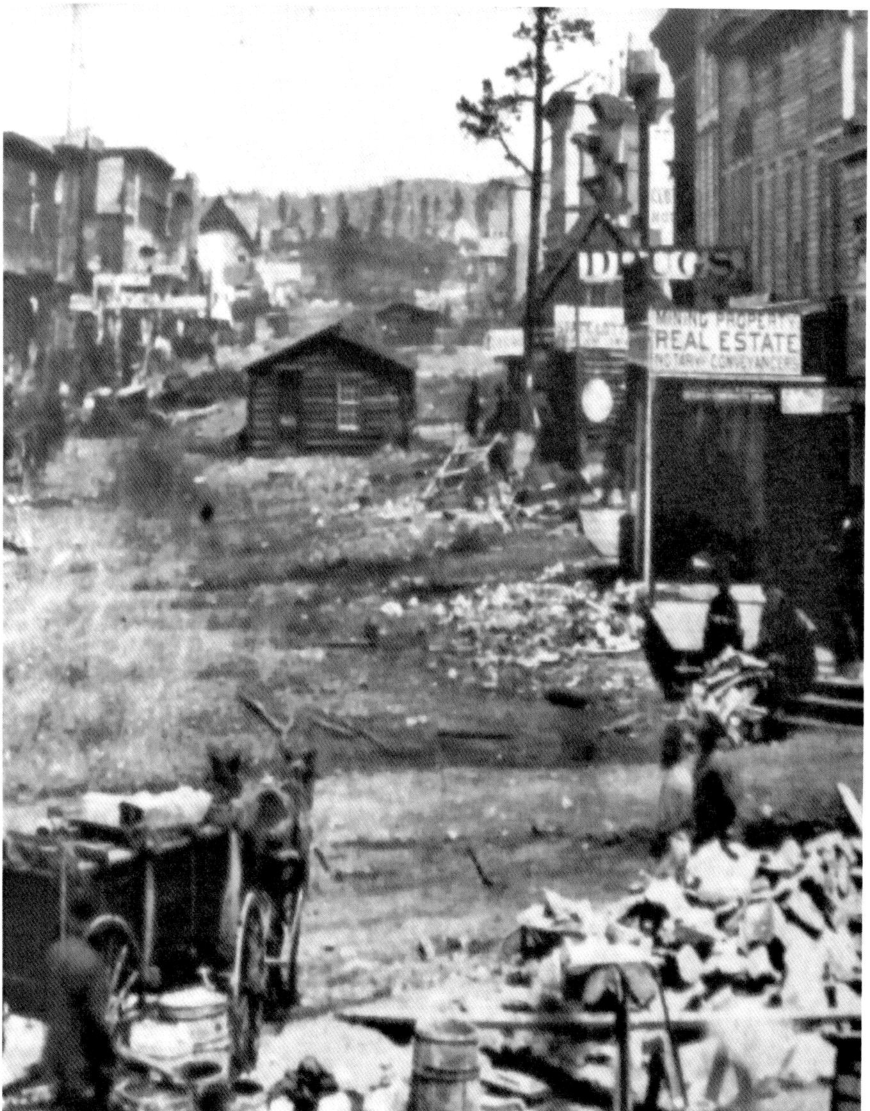

"Pap" Wyman's cabin in the middle of Harrison Avenue about 1879. *Courtesy of the Colorado Mountain History Collection, Lake County Public Library.*

on his dance hall girls. They were allowed to sit on a gentleman's lap to entice him to buy a drink, but the man's hand was not allowed to roam below the lady's neck or above her knee.

Pap dressed in brightly colored shirts and wore flowered vests. Under his real name, C.E. Wyman, he acted in 1882 on the stage of the Grand Central Theater in *Cousin Joe*. Some said that he had a heart of gold. In the morning, before the saloon and theater were cleaned, he invited the local urchins in to search for loose coins that had been carelessly dropped by patrons. Legend says that he was known to purposely drop a few coins himself.

Wyman competed against other saloons, dance halls and theaters by offering his customers a free hot lunch. He converted a small room in the basement to a dining room and served hot lunch three times a day. The menu varied, depending on Pap's taste. On July 4, 1884, he had turtles shipped to Leadville on the train and made green turtle soup as a special treat.

According to Pap, the saloon, theater and dance hall netted him about $50,000 per year. He paid his employees what were considered high wages: bartenders at $150 per month, actors at $75 per week, musicians at $35 per week, female cooks at $25 per month, male cooks at $50 per month and waitresses at $10 per week, plus commissions from the bar.

The theater was located in the rear of the saloon; it was more of a dance hall and variety theater than a legitimate theater. In 1880, the stage was host to Charles Vivian, who performed a successful one-man show. Oscar Wilde wrote about his visit to Pap's when he returned to England.

Pap's saloon and theater was the first in Leadville to be fully lit by electricity. The generators were located in the basement. Early in 1883, Pap traveled to Boston and purchased the necessary equipment. He was excited about the improvement. However, the equipment required a lot of upkeep.

In December, Wyman renovated the theater, upgraded the stage and made other improvements. He reopened with nightly performances by a burlesque troupe of twenty-five beautiful ladies. During the construction of the Carbonate Bank on the northwest corner of Harrison Avenue and Fourth Street, a rumor spread that rich ore was taken out of the site during the excavation and put on display at Wyman's. Crowds flocked to the theater to see the rich ore, only to be shown to the back for the burlesque act, entitled *Specimen Display*. Although duped into spending their hard-earned cash, the men did not complain about the show. Wyman was happy for the rumor; it kept the seats full and the drinks flowing.

Wyman offered better variety, including trapeze artists, than any other variety theater in Leadville. The best way to draw a crowd was to

Wyman's Great Proclamation

IN LEADVILLE, ON CHRISTMAS DAY, DECEMBER 25, 1880.

WHEREAS, I, President of Wyman's business, and being of a sound mind, and having full charge and control of Wyman's business; and

WHEREAS, I have become, by the right of purchase at public sale, of the only and last colored slave in these United States;

I do, in the goodness and greatness of my heart, proclaim his freedom, and that of all other slaves in the United States. And now, to make this contract more pleasant and binding, I do appoint the coming Christmas day, December 25, 1880, at 2 o'clock, p. m., as the day and hour that I do emancipate and set free forever from slavery my last negro, CHARLES GREEN, my lawful property—having been bought by me in the City of Leadville, at public vendue, with my good ducats. But believing that the last fragment of slavery ought to be blotted out from our great and glorious country, I have fully determined as above said. And in order to more fully impress on the minds of this great American people the importance of this great occasion, and the sacred day we celebrate, I do hereby order and demand that all the business houses in this great and wonderful City of Leadville shall be closed at least a few minutes on this great day we celebrate.

And furthermore, I do order a monster procession to be formed in honor of the same in the great City of Leadville. And that it shall consist of all our great and noble societies, including our great County and City Government officers, and all the firemen and other good people, including our colored people especially.

THE PROGRAMME.

From 3 to 4 o'clock a. m., will be set apart as an hour of feasting and prayer, that our citizens and colored people generally may keep in remembrance this great day.

At the conclusion, a marble slab—consisting of a large shingle, appropriately engraved with red chalk—will be erected in front of the new Court House, in commemoration of the immense liberality of our past Board of County Commissioners, with the inscription—"Too Pure for Earth!" Then all the bands will play a beautiful dirge. At this time the audience will stand on their heads, with their feet uncovered, and their hearts bursting with gratitude.

About this time the fire alarm bell in the big tower will be rung 27 seconds, in order to wake up the dance house girls, bunko steerers, tin horn gamblers, and patrons of faro banks.

There will then be a lull in the proceedings, to give all a chance to shake for cocktails. At 5 o'clock a. m., there will be one small fire-cracker fired off in front of the Clarendon Hotel, and 6 o'clock a second-hand sky rocket will be let off in front of the City Jail. Cen. will take charge of this Whereupon all the bells in the city will be thrown to the breeze at half mast, and the flags will ring out their merry peals in honor of the day. The public will please hold their breath while this is going on.

At 7 o'clock Madam Justice, on the new Court House, will make a short address to the great and glorious people of Leadville. After which she declines having any more to do with the business, having recently been vaccinated by a man with his little hatchet, and the government official ordered her removal to Malta, some distance from here, on account of this poisonous altitude.

THE RENDEZVOUS.

At 9 o'clock the different organizations will rendezvous as follows:

The Military in the Tower of the New Court House.

The Masons in the Board of Trade rooms.

The Knights of Pythias in the Grand Central Depot.

The Hibernians in the City Hall

The Good Templars in Jeff. Winney's Temple.

The Firemen in the Grand Central Theatre.

The Odd Fellows in the Methodist belfry.

The Noble Utes in the Tabor Opera House.

The Heathen Chinee outside of the city limits.

The Strikers on Fryer Hill.

The Women's Rights Association on Capitol Hill.

All other societies not herein mentioned will meet at Wyman's free lunch counter for one day's rations.

At 10 o'clock by the sun dog on the postoffice, sooner or later, as Prince says, and that large bodies move slow, the procession will form on Harrison Avenue, the right resting on Wyman's free lunch counter, and will be reviewed by the Mayor and Aldermen, who will then retire for liquid refreshments, previous to firing up for the day. Then the Procesh will meander in the following order:

IN THIS WAY.

Detachment of police mounted on velocipedes.

Band of music.

Then comes the City Government drawn in baby carriages by new milch cows, with a banner of "All that Glitters is not Gold."

Major Potter has kindly volunteered to act as Chief Marshal, and will appear in a carefully prepared collar box drawn by a pair of matched bullfrogs.

Then comes the grand cavalcade, consisting of three vagrants fast asleep waiting for orders to take a drink.

Then a detachment of dead-broke Democrats, who lost their all in the last election, (Wyman will be in that,) headed by the Chalk Ranch Brass Band.

The various Temperance organizations will sit astride beer barrels, and will be drawn by cork screws, headed by Pop.

The lie that Washington told, preserved in a bottle of Wyman's wheat whisky, will be carried by four beautiful virgins from Howard & Sullivan's Black Crook.

The Street Commissioners will be headed by Mike Tierney in person, drawn in whisky barrels. The Fire Department will appear on top, drawn by mules, and anything the City will give them—they will take anything—and will always be on the squirt. The company making the most squirts can take water, or whisky, (at Wyman's).

All the local newspaper reporters will be in a peanut shell, drawn by a batch of lightning bugs, with motto, "People living in glass bottles should not throw stone houses."

The soldiers of the late war will be in a pneumonia ambulance

Then comes the original discoverers of Leadville, all on sorrel horse chestnuts.

Then the bands of the dance houses in single file. After which comes the keno players, tin horn gamblers, sure thing men, and bunko steerers, all mounted on green "bays".

The County Commissioners will be drawn in an egg shell by a jackass in good condition, with a certified pedigree, with banner—"Honesty is the best policy."

The variety show women will be drawn from a champagne bottle, with banner "You must win to please."

The saloon keepers will come to the front, with banner "License must come down."

In the procesh will be an exhibition from Malta—a bag of cats (not two legged on[illegible]

The Malta and Chalk Ranch lighthouses will be brilliantly illuminated during the day with miners' candles.

Owing to the stringency of the money market there will be no general collation served, but all can get a free lunch at Wyman's.

No intoxicating liquors will be sold during the day.

Ladies are requested not to spit tobacco juice on any part of the procession.

There will be a great many preachers in town, and chickens will consult their own interest by roosting very high.

As a great many visitors may be left over from Denver and other small towns, arrangements have been made for extra bunks in the private boxes of the Grand Central Theatre.

All stragglers and groggy persons will be run in as vagrants, but Wyman won't buy any more of them at auction.

A beautiful banner will be presented to the liberated slave by 24 young ladies in white (wash).

A beautiful banner will be carried by 13 of the most beautiful young ladies in Leadville and Malta, with the inscription "What is home without a mother (in-law)."

THE LINE OF MARCH,

In which all are invited to join, without regard to race, color or previous condition, will be headed by the freed slave, and will start at 12 o'clock, m., and will march directly to Wyman's to help get away with the one hundred baskets of wines and liquors given by Mr. Wyman in honor of the great event. After that the procesh will move in the following order: via the depot to the brewery, where they will halt a few minutes and take a few kegs of beer aboard, thence to Chalk Ranch via the Arkansas River in boats, each boat being well provided with life preservers; thence to Kokomo, where they will take a small lunch; from there only a short distance to the summit of Mount of the Holy Cross, where one of our most particular friends and near neighbors has kindly consented to deliver the oration. I have reference to that noble piece of humanity the Great Ute, during which time all will uncover. After which the line of march will be taken up via the Soda Springs and Malta to the place of beginning, where Wyman will then make a short speech, giving his experience as a slave holder.

After which everybody is expected to repair to their virtuous and quiet homes.

C. E. WYMAN,
The last of the slaveholders.

Satire published by "Pap" Wyman in 1880. *Courtesy of the Colorado Mountain History Collection, Lake County Public Library.*

advertise the danger. Audiences were excited because there was no safety net. They got to see just how dangerous it could be in January 1885 when Lon Eddy performed. The ceiling rod that held the trapeze broke, and Lon came crashing toward the stage. Fortunately, the safety harness grabbed him, but it cut a large gash in Lon's side. Although injured, he gave everyone a show by climbing up the rope to the ceiling, blood dripping from his wound, to unhook the harness, and then he climbed back down to the stage floor on another rope.

In the spring of 1887, Pap turned over the management to Julius Kolsh and William Cowan and moved to Denver to concentrate on his saloon, dance hall and theater there. The Leadville saloon remained open and operated in the same manner as when Pap was in charge. The theater and dance hall lost favor and were closed shortly after Kolsh and Cowan were put in charge.

Carbonate Concert Hall

The Carbonate Concert Hall, located at State and the northwest corner of Pine Streets, opened on June 9, 1879. The owner, J.F. Stockdorf, was known in Denver as a first-class hotelier. His partner and manager was Gus Vogus. The building was forty-eight by seventy-five feet, sixteen feet to the plate and thirty feet high in the center. The entrance had a large Gothic-style window in the front, giving it the look of a cathedral. Living pine trees were planted along the walls inside the building. On the north end was the stage, with large oil paintings hanging above it. On cloudy and cold days, it was heated with coal oil furnaces and lit with coal oil chandeliers. The hall could seat 150, with an additional 50 people at tables. It offered free music and entertainment daily. Beer brewed in Leadville was on tap, while the best bottled wines were available in bottles.

Stockdorf closed the hall for remodeling the following year. When he reopened, he advertised new kalsomine paint made of slaked lime (calcium hydroxide), the equivalent of whitewashing in the most elegant style, and the hall was lit by Japanese lanterns. It offered the best talent, Buck Beer on draught and Sunday afternoon concerts performed by sixteen of Leadville's best artists. On June 20, 1880, the Lady Vienna Orchestra played here, thought to be the best show ever held at this hall. The performance could not save this theater, though, and it was soon closed.

In 1881, the hall was reopened, operated by John Eitel, and during his management, it gained the reputation of a respectable place of amusement. Admission was free, as Eitel made his money off the bar, and the drinks flowed freely. He made sure that the peace was kept during his reign and that he did not have the same problems as many of the other State Street dives.

One newspaper noted that "immoral females" were waitresses at his establishment. After an incident in February 1881, Eitel threw a drunken man out of his business. He petitioned the city council to appoint Jo Jones as a special policeman in charge of the Carbonate Hall. The city felt that Eitel needed all the help he could get because they approved the motion. Eitel did have to pay Jones's salary, however.

In January 1883, John Eitel took advantage of what he called "the manly art." He remodeled the theater to fit a boxing ring on the stage, tore out the old floor and added a new floor that could hold the punishments of sport. New boxes were added that increased privacy for the patrons. Eitel then began booking the best boxing, wrestling and gymnastic bouts in Leadville as part of the variety at the theater.

Police Gazette Palace

In November, the theater was leased to Harry Webb, who changed the name to the Police Gazette Palace and ran it with a wrestling and boxing venue. On opening night, Webb announced the upcoming fight on November 20 between Tom "Coal Creek Champion" Walling and Mike "the Brooklyn Boy" Haley for a $250 prize.

When the two men fought, Walling easily won in the fourth round. Many of the patrons of the theater accused Haley, believed to be the favorite, of drinking before going into the ring.

Webb also announced that Ada DeAlvin was willing to fight any female in Colorado for a $100 purse. DeAlvin worked at the theater as a trapeze artist and a female fighter. She took a bad fall off the trapeze one night and suffered pain for months before dying of a morphine overdose in January 1884.

In September 1884, Milton Charles, a former police officer, took over the management. He brought in variety actors in from the East Coast. Milton paid the train fare for a certain female performer to come to Leadville and perform at the Police Gazette Palace. When she arrived, she met Mike Goldsmith, who was running the Liberty Hall. He told her that Charles was a swindler and a pauper and not in the habit of paying salaries. Then Goldsmith offered her a job at the Liberty Hall.

A few nights later, Goldsmith wandered into the Police Gazette Palace to gloat about his new talent. Charles ordered him to leave. Goldsmith refused and pulled out a knife. Charles demanded to be paid for the train fare, picked up a beer bottle and threw it at Goldsmith. Both were arrested and hauled into court. Charles said, "Goldsmith did not treat me right, in fact he acted like a cur towards me." They were fined for breach of peace. These two theater managers seemed bent on destroying each other in competing to be the best variety theater in town.

The McDaniel's New Theater

James McDaniel returned to Leadville in the winter of 1886, looking to open another theater. He went into business for a short period with Laura LeClair, but this did not last long. He found the Old Carbonate Hall was empty. He purchased the building and changed the name to the McDaniel's New Theater. A reporter asked why he chose to return to Leadville. He replied that he had grown tired of traveling and wanted to find a solid town where he could make some money. Leadville looked like the right place.

On opening night, June 1, 1886, more than one thousand people crowded in to celebrate the return of an old friend. McDaniel had earned the nickname "the Barnum of the West," which was fitting, as Barnum's circus was where he got his start. The theater was reported to be the best vaudeville house west of the Mississippi. McDaniel completely remodeled the building in an elegant fashion, and the bar was stocked with the choicest liquors and cigars. He operated the theater as a variety theater, offering a collection of different acts, one of the most popular being the trapeze act by Will and Minnie known as "The Celebrated Ricketts." McDaniel sold the theater to Mike Goldsmith a few months later. Goldsmith changed the name to Carbonate Theater.

Carbonate Theater

Mike Goldsmith hired John Tudor, of the famous Leadville and Aspen acting family, to manage the theater. Goldsmith advertised with such phrases as "Unequalled Entertainment," "Always on the lookout for acts that attract and interest the amusement-going public," "The result of the public patronage at the Carbonate Theater is simply immense," "First-class people engaged to appear" and "Everything Goes."

Goldsmith also offered boxing matches, and on December 24, 1886, more than one thousand people came to see some of the best boxers of the time: world champ John Sullivan, George "the Fighting Marine" La Blanche, former U.S. title holder Steve Taylor, New England champ Jim Carroll and Duncan McDonald, champion of the Northwest.

Many of these men had fought in Leadville before, but to have all of them on one stage at the same time was impressive. The audience got to see why Sullivan was the champion; he took on both McDonald and Taylor in four rounds each and was declared the winner in both. After the fight, a reporter interviewed Sullivan and asked him how he felt. He replied, "Much better than three years ago; when I was here before, I was drinking all the time. Now I am not drinking at all."

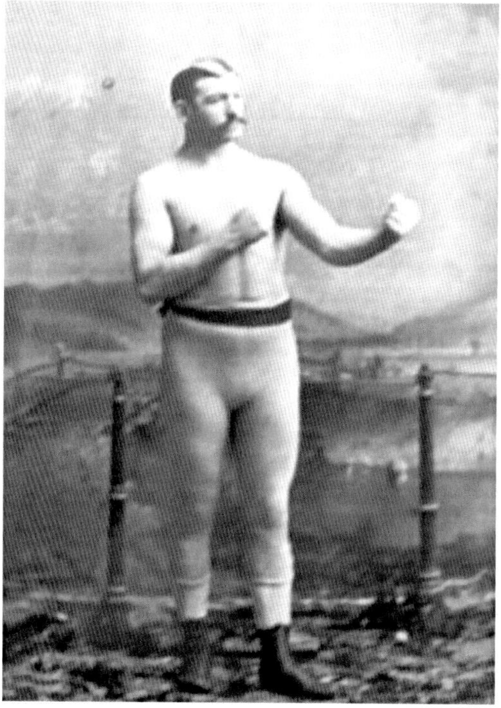

John Sullivan.

Although Goldsmith wanted to advertise that the theater was for everyone, it had the same reputation as any other theater on State Street. One incident happened when Charles Lederman came to have a good time and met Minnie Whistler, a State Street lady known to do business in the theater. Charles thought that the attention was love, and so he took her to his apartment. The next morning, Charles found that his love was gone, along with his wallet and eighty dollars. The police arrested her; as a final insult, she used Charles's money to post bail.

In the fall of 1888, Goldsmith expanded the programming, offering a Sunday Night Hop, similar to the attractions of the dance halls. He also hired the prettiest dancers in town. One evening, a local dance hall owner came over and offered to buy the patrons a drink. Shouts of joy ran out. The crowd gathered around the bar, and he boasted about cheaper drinks at his place, encouraging the men to go there. The crowd became smaller as the men left to check out the other dance hall. He began passing out cash to the remaining patrons, enticing them to leave. Goldsmith arrived later, to an empty house, and wept. The next morning, he posted a notice to all dance hall owners, stating that they were not welcome in his hall.

Goldsmith sold the theater to Ben Loeb in December 1888. Loeb combined the management of this theater with the Central Theater, employing the same actors at both.

The City Hall

I.W. Chatfield built this three-story, pine-framed building in 1880 at 134–136 East Sixth Street. The first floor was retail space—a restaurant where meals cost thirty-five cents on one side and a saloon in the other. The second floor was fitted as a large hall, with the finest dance floor. It could be rented for any type of entertainment or rally. Apartments were on the third floor.

Chatfield was running for city council, and maybe that is why he named the building the "City Hall." It was hailed as the largest hall in Colorado, holding more than six hundred people. Opening day, April 14, 1880, the Episcopalian Ladies club held a three-day bazaar.

For a time, the First Christian Church used the hall for Sunday services under Reverend U.M. Browder. Reverend Mackey of St. George's Episcopal Church also reserved the hall one evening per week. He held temptation-free socials for those wishing to avoid the sins of gambling and drinking. One had to sign a pledge and was given a card that said he or she was a member of Lcadville Anti-Treating Society:

> *I herby solemnly promise that, for a period of one year from this date.*
> *I will neither treat nor be treated to any kind of alcoholic or malt liquors.*
> ______________________________ *Signed* __________________
> *Witnesses By* ______________________ *dated* ____________________

In July, the Presbyterians booked the hall for guest lecturer Reverend Thomas De Witt Talmage, a fiery, well-known preacher from Brooklyn,

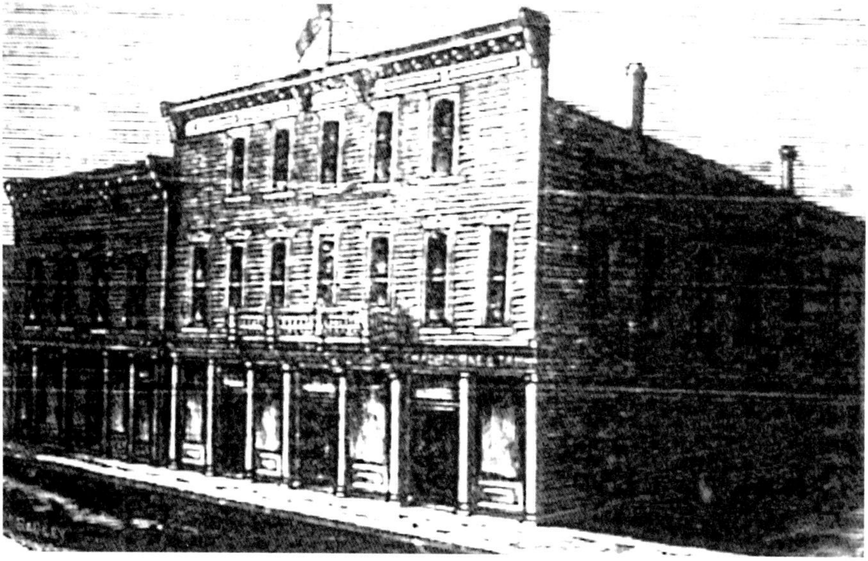

Line drawing of City Hall, from the *Herald Democrat*.

New York. Many preachers visited the seedier side of New York at night and built that experience into the Sunday sermon, preaching about the sin on their own streets.

When Talmage and his wife arrived in Leadville, the Clarendon Hotel placed them in a room on the ground floor but the next day offered to move them to Governor Pitkin's room. Talmage said that they would take both rooms so he would not wake his wife when he went on his nightly walks.

After his lecture at City Hall, he returned to the hotel, leaving again at about 11:00 p.m. He and a companion wandered down the street into the Board of Trade Saloon, the Wyman Saloon and the Texas House—all to see the seedier side of Leadville. While at the Wyman, Reverend Talmage noticed the Bible near the door and took time to preach to the crowd. On State Street, he stopped at the Odeon Dance Hall and the Red Light Dance Hall. At the Odeon, the manager asked Talmage if he would like a lady for the dance; Talmage politely refused. While in the dance hall, Talmage timidly inquired if all men in Leadville carried firearms. He hoped to get a view of Leadville's famous female gambler Kitty Crawhurst, but she was not there.

When he returned to his New York pulpit, he said, "Leadville is the most lied about city in the west, sure it has its wickedness on the surface, but there are more murders in Brooklyn than in Leadville. Their churches are crowded on Sunday."

In 1881, Annunciation Catholic Church held its annual bazaar at the hall. It made an unprecedented $10,000. One lady's hat sold for $2,000. A popular dance hall girl had been talking to the gamblers in the saloon where she worked about how much she liked the hat. Some of them went to the auction and started a bidding war; the hat was valued at less than $5.

On March 3, 1889, a horseshoe-making contest between David Moore and Jack Hill was held on the stage at the hall. Moore bet $100 that he could make one hundred horseshoes before Hill could make eighty-two. Flaming forges were placed on the stage, and showers of sparks flew as the blacksmiths worked. Firefighters were present, in case one of the embers caught the stage on fire. After two hours, Hill had made eighty-three shoes, while Moore had only made seventy-six whole shoes and nineteen halves. Hill won the $100.

Live chess was an interesting benefit event held by the Presbyterian church on April 7, 1889. The stage floor was marked off in a blue and white chessboard pattern. Pawns were played by young schoolgirls, while the large pieces were played by teens and adults. Everyone was told where to move by the players. At the beginning, the pieces did an elaborate march to their places on the board while the Orpheus Club Orchestra played "March of the Priests."

Each piece was dressed in an elaborate costume, made of the finest silk and velvet and decorated with gold, lace and jewels, all of which was purchased in Denver a week earlier. The royalty of the game was adorned in the best costumes and diamonds, valued at $12,000 and lent to them by leading jewelers in Denver and Leadville. The event was a combination of a play and the game of chess. Although live chest tournaments had been played in Colorado before, none had been played with such detail to the costumes.

In 1890, one of the biggest attractions was not on stage, but on display in the City Hall Saloon. "Doc" Burkhardt and E.A. Hanifer, manager of the saloon, purchased a chicken from a traveling man for five dollars. The hen looked like a chicken except for its head. "It had a red head that looked like a snake, and when angered by the bartender poking it with a stick, its head snapped back and mouth opened, and out came a forked tongue. Unlike a snake, it had full red lips and a row of tiny teeth." The chicken was unable to peck at grain, so it was fed bread, which it chewed. Crowds of people came to the bar every day to see the chicken.

On April 1, 1891, Ben Loeb brought his novelty acts to the hall. One popular act was Libbie Ross, a female pugilist and one of America's first female boxers. Female boxing began in 1876 in New York at Harry Hill's Variety Theater. In 1880, the National Police Gazette announced that Libbie Ross was the champion female boxer, after her victory over Carrie Edwards at Harry Hill's. Libbie took her show on the road, eventually ending up in Leadville.

The hall was best known for its grand evening balls. The grandest were held there by every of social club in Leadville. During the Hard Times Ball, held annually (the first was on March 22, 1888) at City Hall, the ladies dressed in calico primitive-style dresses and the men in their oldest and rattiest clothes.

An advertisement for the Hard Times Ball in 1889 noted:

> *You pay 99-cents to go to the Hard Times Ball, wear your smelting clothes and ride in your slag cart.*
> *You may dance all you want, provided your feet don't get sore and your shoe leather lasts.*
> *Prof. Simons will tell what you are supposed to dance and you may take your lunch along in a tin dinner pail.*

For the masquerade balls, the most creative themes and the best costumes were seen. When the railroad switchmen held their ball on June 10, 1891, they decorated the hall with railroad lanterns and live evergreen trees. On October 25, 1892, the firemen took over the hall for their fourth annual ball. An alarm system was placed in the hall—the firemen needed to be alerted if there was a fire. It was decorated with items from their everyday life: fire hoses used as bunting, ladders placed around the hall, axes crossed above the threshold and alarms used as a centerpiece.

The Elks Lodge held one of the oddest events, the Pound Ball, on April 1, 1894. Instead of a grand march, gentlemen marched their dates on stage, where everyone guessed each lady's weight. The lady was weighed, and everyone paid one and a half cents for every pound they were off; whoever guessed the closest won the money. Prizes were given for the heaviest women at 210 pounds and the lightest at 60 pounds. The total weight of the ladies that night was 21,000 pounds. None of the gentlemen were weighed.

City Hall was not immune to the pull of the money brought in by boxing and wrestling matches. In a fight between the "Montana" Kid and Jack Davis, more than 1,500 people crowded in the hall. While the people of the crowd cheered, yelled and stomped their feet, the floor began to sag. Suddenly, the floor dropped six inches, and the crowd panicked. Everyone rushed out, threatening to trample anyone in their way. A few quick-thinking volunteers took to the stage and called for order, so the remainder could exit safely.

Rollaway Rink

In 1909, the City Hall was opened for a short time as the Rollaway Rink. The top two floors were condemned and deemed unsafe for events; the old pine siding had dried up and cracked in the sun. For many years, a saloon operated on the ground floor, but soon it, too, was moved to a better location. The building was empty except for one tenant, who was also the caretaker. It was part of the Wilson family estate and looked as though it would be torn down and the lots sold off.

In the early morning of April 2, 1916, the fire alarms rang. The firemen rushed to East Sixth Street to find that both the Grove and O'Keefe Wallpaper and Paint Store and the City Hall were on fire. The caretaker was living on the third floor and escaped through a window. The fire was quickly doused, and the firemen went to breakfast at a local restaurant.

While they were eating, the wind picked up, stirring up some of the smoldering embers. The firemen quickly returned to the burning buildings and called their volunteers, including the Camp Hale Fire Department, to assist. People ran up and down the street, in the path of the fire, trying to help. Coffins were pulled out of the Moynahan & O'Malia Funeral Home storage and lined up in the street, with harnesses, tack and horses from the B.H. Martin Livery Stable. Soon, the street was littered with rescued goods, coffins, broken glass and burning embers.

An overzealous telegraph operator sent out reports—reaching as far away as New York—that the whole town was on fire. Soon, it became evident that if the fire department didn't do something quickly, it might become the truth. The decision was made to dynamite the buildings, including the City Hall, causing the street to fill with smoke, backing the fire department off

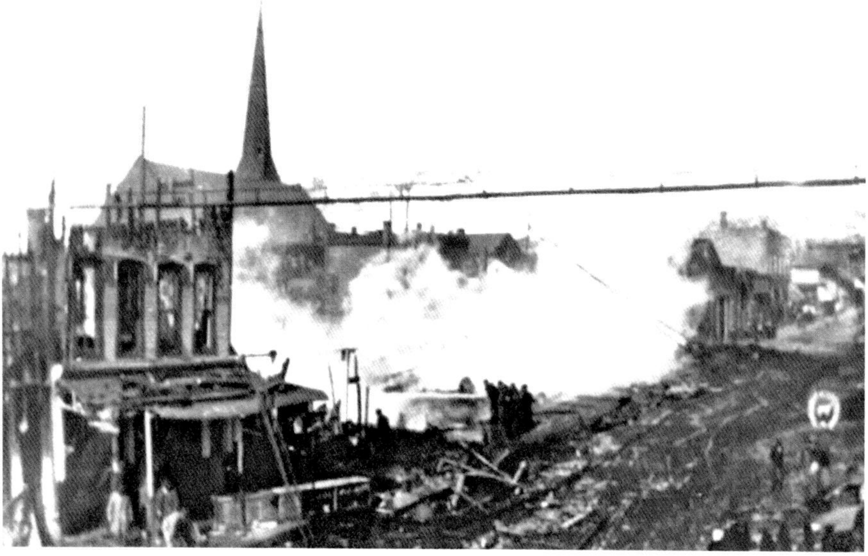

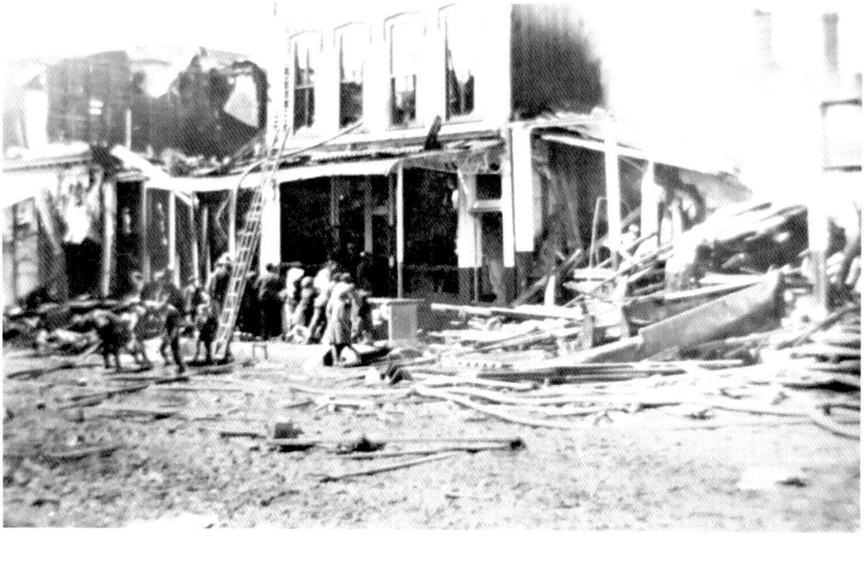

An April 2, 1916 fire burned City Hall and other buildings on East Sixth Street. *Courtesy of the Colorado Mountain History Collection, Lake County Public Library.*

the block for several minutes. When the smoke cleared, they were able to get the fire under control.

Twelve buildings were lost that day. The City Hall was empty and belonged to the Wilson estate. It was valued at $1,000. The loss for all twelve buildings was more than $50,000. The cause was never discovered. There were rumors that a Wilson estate beneficiary was responsible, or possibly it was caused by chemicals improperly stored in a back room.

The vacant lots were purchased by the Cloud City Amusement Company, which built the Cloud City Skating Rink in 1917. It served a variety of uses, including for vaudeville performances, as a dance hall to raise money for the Soldiers Smokers Fund during World War I and as a gym until 1923. This building is still standing and in use as the Sixth Street Gym.

The Iris Theater

This theater was located at 517–519 Harrison Avenue, formerly operated as a little vaudeville theater named Congress Hall and the Empire Theater. By 1909, the name had changed again, to the Iris Theater. On October 31, 1912, hypnotist J.P. Caruthers took the stage and said that he was looking for a young boy to be hypnotized. Tony Zalar, a youngster with a reputation for trouble, agreed for ten dollars. Tony was put into a deep sleep and put on a stationary bike in the pool hall window at Seventh and Harrison.

For one day, Tony pedaled the bike as large crowds gathered outside. Some women felt that this was cruel, so they complained to Mayor Rose. He went to see the boy and demanded that he be woken up. Caruthers refused, saying that he would be woken up the next day in front of an audience. The mayor called for the police, who told Caruthers to wake up the boy or he would go to jail. Caruthers laughed and refused to wake him up.

The mayor became more upset and called for a doctor, who felt that Tony was fine, just in a deep sleep. The boy was laid on a cot and moved to the theater. Meanwhile, a crowd gathered; the mayor refused to allow Caruthers to charge admission. He was finally taken to jail. Not sure what to do with the sleeping boy, the mayor moved Tony to Caruthers's cell. The mayor insisted that no bail would be set until he woke up the boy.

The next day, Caruthers pleaded his case in court and was fined twenty-five dollars for exhibiting without a license and for resisting arrest. Even though the theater had a license, the court noted that it did not extend to the pool hall. Caruthers appealed the ruling, stating that he was employed by the theater and that the license should have covered him. Also, the police did not arrest him for exhibiting but because they thought the boy was in danger. The case and the fines were dismissed, the court having decided that it was the mayor's abuse of power that led to the arrest. Caruthers woke Tony from his sleep, and both left the jail.

In December, Caruthers sued the city, Mayor Rose and the Leadville Police Department for $25,400 for assault, wrongful arrest, refusal of bond and prohibiting him from making a living here. He stated that when he was arrested, two officers threw him off the stage. When he asked for a physician, they refused. Also, the city was not allowing him to make a living, and by morally disgracing him, he could not get a job elsewhere.

The court decided in favor of J.B. Caruthers, stating that the city and the marshal interfered with his right to put on a good show and falsely arrested him. The judge also stated that placing the boy in the window was not breaking the city's code on having a license to hold an exhibit; the fault belonged to Mayor Rose, and the marshal was just following orders. The judge did not believe that Caruthers experienced serious injury during his arrest; however, he awarded him $297 plus court costs.

The New Grand Theater

In 1913, the name was now the New Grand Theater, and in 1915, the theater sued the Musicians Protective Association for $1,000 because the theater fired the orchestra fiddler. The association felt that it was a violation of his contract, which noted that no musician could be fired without two weeks' notice. The theater said that the fiddler left in the middle of a performance and refused to return, so they fired him. The association put the New Grand on an "unfair list" and threatened other theaters if they entered into business with the New Grand.

The association also wanted a pay raise. The theater had raised admission to $0.10 per person, and the musicians wanted their cut. At the time, the orchestra leader was paid $21.00 per week and the sidemen $17.50 per week. Theaters also had to abide by other restrictions: they could not employ fewer than three musicians, and one must be a leader. They were allowed to play for three hours per night and no more than two matinees per day, and performances could not be longer than one hour forty minutes. The judge determined the theater had grounds to fire the fiddler, and a raise only needed to be discussed at the contract renewal.

The issue of salaries raised its ugly head again in 1917, when the Musicians Protective Association approved a fifty-cent-per-night raise for musicians without consulting the theaters. The association demanded the theater pay the new wage or the musicians would refuse to play. The three major movie houses refused to pay; the Industry Commission was called in to settle the dispute.

One day before the musicians were scheduled to walk out, the Industry Commission asked the musicians to wait until it had made a decision. The theaters held firm. They could not pay the raise to $24.50 for leaders and $21.00 for sidemen. Later that year, the theaters raised the admission from $0.10 to $0.15 in order to pay the salaries of additional musicians the union required.

Liberty Bell Theater

The International Amusement Company, under the ownership of Henry Goodridge, planned this building on the northwest corner of Sixth and Harrison Avenue, opening two years later on January 5, 1919. The company also owned the Ogden, the York and Thompson Theaters in Denver. The lot cost $5,000. A two-story frame building that housed a grocery store and tailor shop was razed to make way for the new building. This site was chosen because of the slope of the lot, giving it the right pitch for the theater floor incline. It was an investment for locals, as stock certificates were sold before the opening.

The two-story brick building, 36 by 124 feet, was fireproof and had very modern lighting, heating and ventilation systems. It could seat 750 people. The cost for this state-of-the-art theater was $25,000. The company chose Leadville because of the large number of stockholders here. It was considered one of the finest, well-equipped moving picture theaters in Colorado.

Films arrived in Leadville the same way actors did: aboard the train. The manager booked films three to four weeks in advance. Reels were copied and sent to Denver. They had to cover all of Colorado, Wyoming, New Mexico and parts of Texas. If a film did not make the Leadville train, it would rebook it for a later date.

The Liberty occasionally hosted stage performances. In March 1919, Josef D'Harvarda, a famous French master violinist, was engaged at the Liberty Bell for one week. He played to a packed house every night.

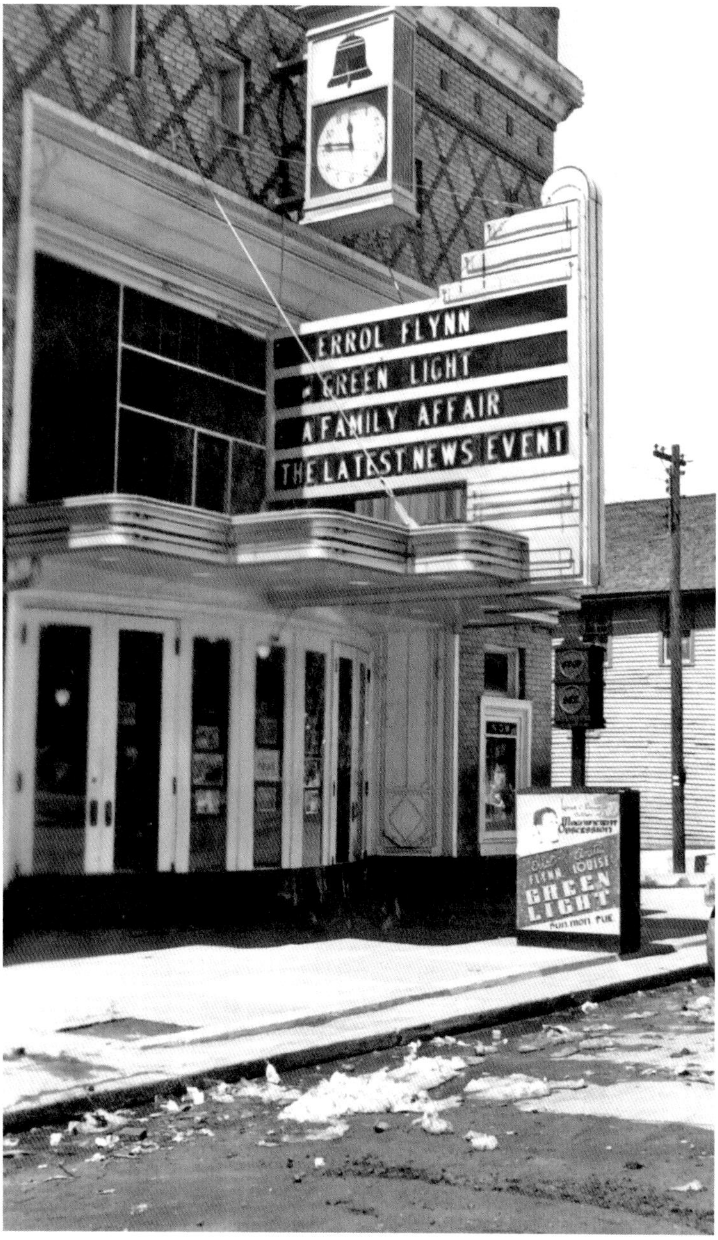

This page and following two pages: Advertising movies at the Fox Theater. *Courtesy of the Colorado Mountain History Collection, Lake County Public Library.*

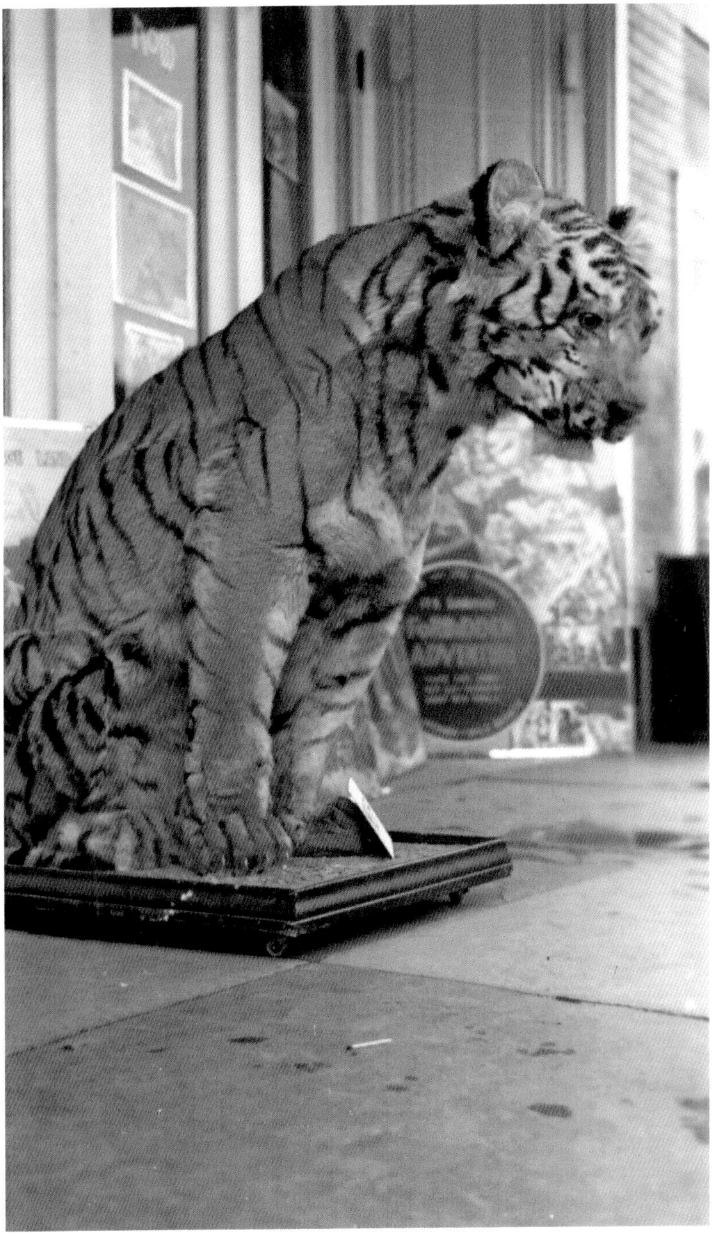

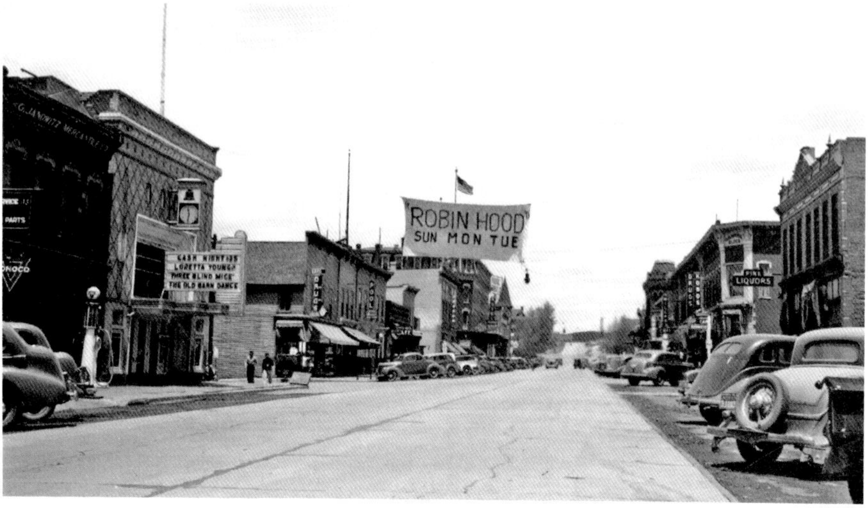

The Liberty was always looking for the newest technology to improve the movie watching experience. In 1921, it upgraded the production booth, adding a second projector, allowing staff to change reels without interruption. The film ran through the projectors at an average rate of one thousand feet in fifteen minutes. The projectors had lights so large and strong that if light escaped through a break in the film for more than six seconds, it could cause a fire in the production booth.

The projectors stood side by side on a cork base to absorb vibration. Due to the fire hazard from the projectors' lights and heat, the booth was lined with steel and had steel trapdoors. The doors were held open by pulleys and ropes, with rings holding the rope and pulleys up. The rings were designed to melt in intense heat or fire, leading the doors to slam closed and protecting the auditorium from fire.

The Fox Theater

The Liberty Bell became part of the Fox Theater Circuit on August 1, 1935, and the name changed to the Fox Theater. There was also a two-hundred-

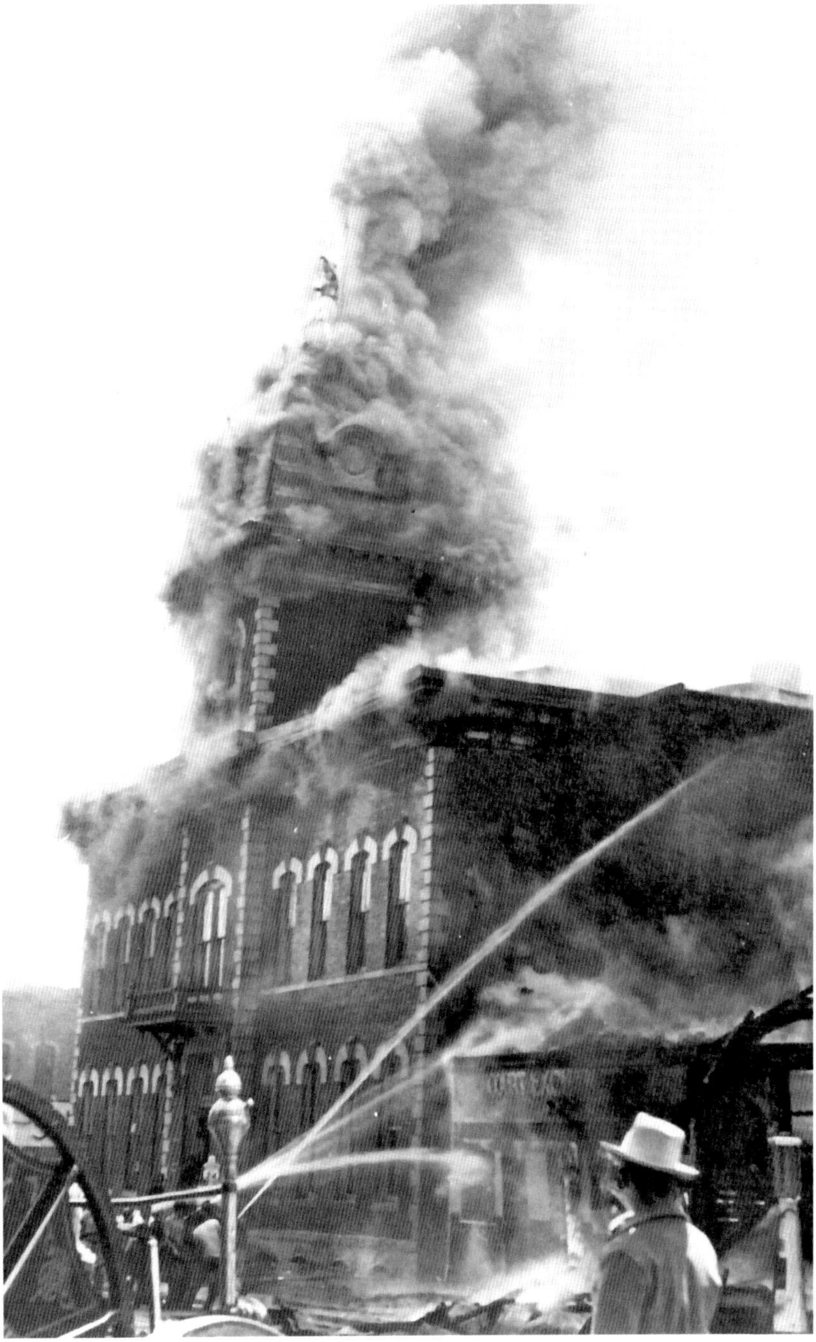

Courthouse fire, June 29, 1942. *Author's collection.*

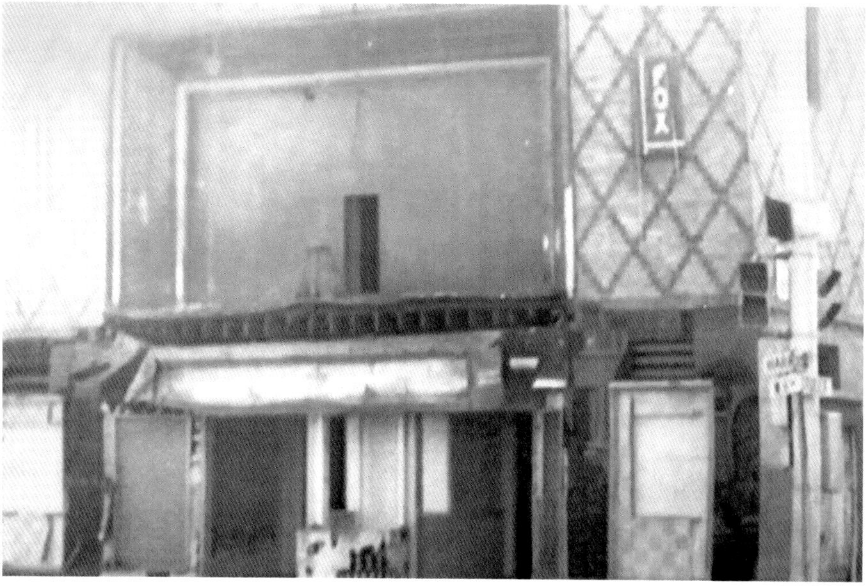

Fox Theater shortly before it was torn down.

seat Fox Theater at Climax, and the Tabor Opera House was part of the Fox Theater Circuit in the 1940s.

On June 29, 1942, the employees were burning trash, popcorn boxes and paper in oil barrels behind the theater. The fire was not watched carefully, and it caused Boyton's garage next door to catch fire. Considerable damage was done, but the theater refused to pay for the damages. The garage owners sued; however, the judge found in the favor of the theater.

The Fox Theater continued to operate until 1963. It was in need of repairs and was costly to operate. The Lake County commissioners purchased the building in order to use it for county offices. After obtaining the bids for the remodel, they decided that it was more cost effective to build new county offices, and the building was torn down and replaced with a parking lot.

Tabor Opera House

The original contract for this building was \$30,000. J.T. Roberts, the contractor, broke ground on August 1, 1879, and sold the contract to L.E. Roberts soon after. The total cost amounted to more than \$75,000. Although H.A.W. Tabor is given credit for the opera house, the initial contract was made by William Bush, owner of the Clarendon Hotel, with the Leadville Brick Company to build this building. Tabor owned the land and was an initial investor.

Before ground could be broken, the home of Horace and Augusta Tabor had to be moved from 300 Harrison Avenue. The house was jacked up, logs were positioned underneath and a team of horses rolled the house to East Fifth Street, where it resides today.

Later, Bush ran out of money. He went to his friend Tabor for more money to finish. Tabor invested more and more, and soon the two friends had worked out an agreement: it would be the Tabor Opera House instead of the Bush Opera House. Bush's connection explains why the third floor was used as additional rooms for the Clarendon, with a walkway between the two buildings.

Tabor bought Bush out of his investments, but Bush didn't feel that he had been treated fairly. He later purchased the Broadway Theater in Denver, near the Tabor Grand Opera House, becoming Tabor's biggest competitor. All seemed fair since Tabor built the Vendome Hotel in Leadville, in direct competition with the Clarendon Hotel.

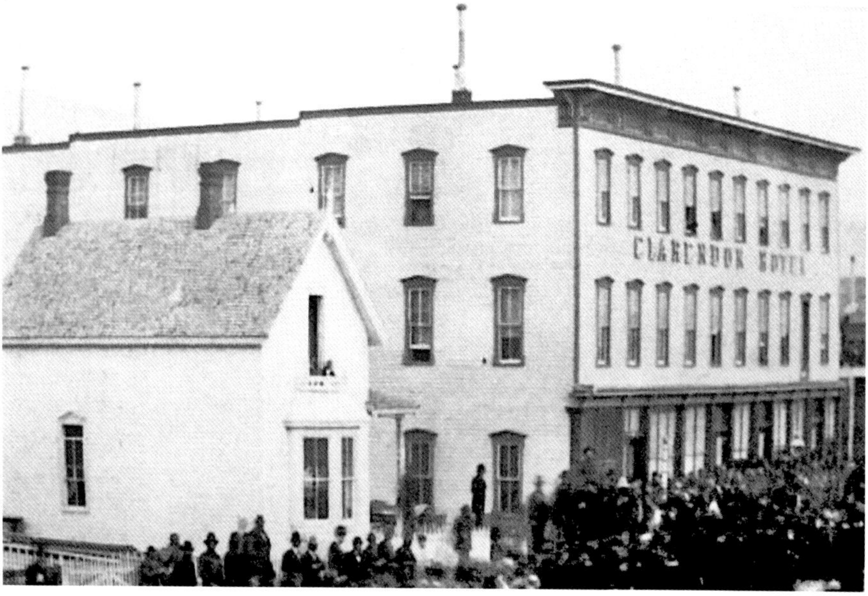

The original Tabor home on Harrison Avenue before it was moved to East Fifth Street to make room for the Tabor Opera House in 1878. *Courtesy of the Colorado Mountain History Collection, Lake County Public Library.*

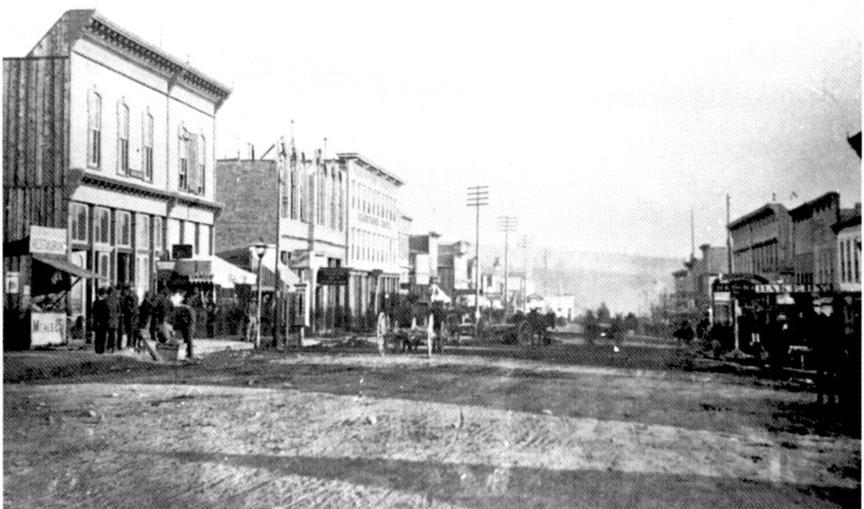

The partially built Tabor Opera House in 1879. *Courtesy of the Colorado Mountain History Collection, Lake County Public Library.*

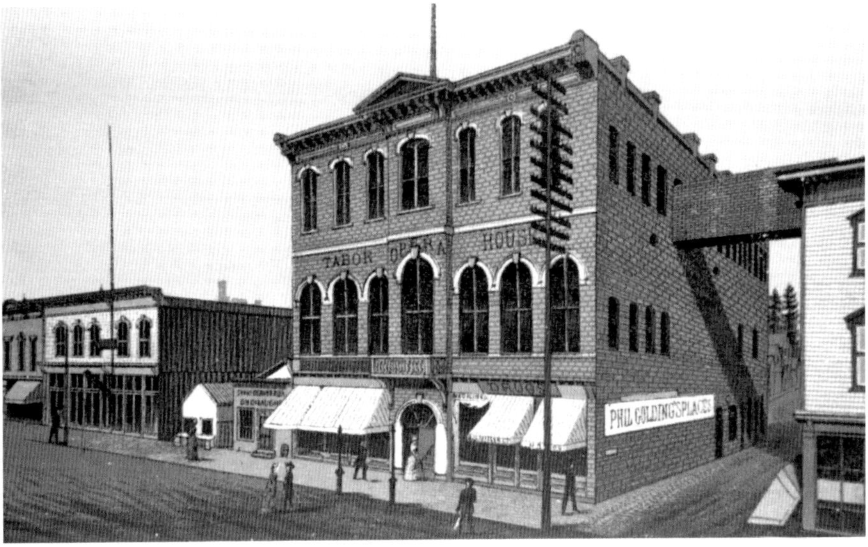

Postcard depiction of the Tabor Opera House.

The opera house opened 102 days after groundbreaking. It was described as a three-story brick structure, trimmed with Portland cement, with frontage on the avenue of sixty feet, extending back one hundred feet. The ground floor had two spacious storefronts—the north one was Sands, Pelton & Company, and the south was the J.S. Miller Drug Store. The windows for the Sands, Pelton store arrived on October 1, 1879. They were six by eleven feet, the largest panes of glass to come by wagon over Mosquito Pass. The contractor insisted that they be installed quickly so nothing happened to them; work was finished in thirty minutes without mishap.

Sands, Pelton had stores in Black Hawk and Central City. Jake Sands was a friend of Elizabeth "Baby" Doe, a young lady he brought to Leadville from Central City to start a new life after her divorce from Harvey Doe. Some said that he wanted her to become his wife, but she would soon become a part of one of the biggest scandals of her time when she caught the eye of Horace Tabor. Tabor later divorced Augusta to marry the blue-eyed beauty.

A ten-foot staircase, in the middle of the two stores, led to the second-floor audience rooms. In the back of the stores was a wareroom, used as the commissary department for the Clarendon; later, this became Phil Golding's Saloon.

In the front of the second floor were several rooms—two on the left were Tabor's, while the other three were Bush's. The theater was also located on the second floor, and a hallway separated the rooms from the audience. A six-foot double door in the middle led to the seating, with two three-foot doorways on either side.

The auditorium was fifty-seven by sixty-seven feet deep, with a two-foot incline of the floor, toward the back. The stage was thirty-four feet deep, running the width of the room and rising above the theater seats, and it had an incline of six inches. The Andrew Make seats were cast iron, with scarlet crushed-velvet upholstery. The walls and ceiling were frescoed and brightly colored.

Small staircases led from the main floor to a horseshoe-shaped dress circle that extended around the room. The main floor seated 450 people, and the dress circle sat 400 more. There were two proscenium boxes on either side of the stage, with lambrequin lace curtains. Bush employed Mr. Barber as stage carpenter, considered one of the best in the business, having designed stages in New York City.

The stage held thirty gaslights, and fine scene designer J.E. Lamphier painted some of the best scenes in theaters in New York and Pennsylvania. The drop curtain, also painted by Lamphier, was a mountain scene with a castle at the base alongside a stream and road. A few years later, Tabor contracted to have a new drop curtain painted by Gene Field. Lore says that the first design was a portrait of Shakespeare. When Tabor saw the design, he asked, "Who is that man?" Field replied, "Shakespeare." Tabor laughed, and said, "What did Shakespeare do for Colorado? If you want to paint a portrait, it should be one of me."

Field's next design was the Royal Gorge, and it was ultimately painted for the curtain; it was still being used when the Elks enlarged the stage in 1902. It was taken down, and there was a great deal of debate over what should happen to it. Some thought that it should be hung in the Carnegie Library or donated to the Leadville Pioneers for safekeeping; others thought that the main part should be cut out, framed and hung in the opera house.

The curtain stayed at the opera house. In 1932, it was lent to the Denver Theater for the premiere of the movie *Silver Dollar*, starring Edward G. Robinson, based on Tabor's life. What happened to the curtain after this remains a mystery. It may have been returned to the opera house and placed in the attic, along with many of the other discarded scenes and curtains, waiting to be restored.

The third floor had twenty-five rooms, with a closed walkway between the Clarendon and opera house for guests to access their rooms without traveling though the opera house.

Tabor and Bush hired Jack Langrishe as the manager. His troupe, with Phosa McAllister as the lead actress, was the main performer. Before the railroad, traveling troupes were few and far between, and the cost to bring a show to Leadville would have far exceeded the revenue.

Traveling companies had to concentrate on performing one to two plays, memorizing those lines. Stock companies performed a show one night, learned the lines for a new show the next day and performed the new show that night. They were always presenting the newest and most exciting plays available.

The building would officially open a month later, but the first event was held on October 3, 1879. The Ladies Catholic Church Fair was held on the ground floor, even before the upper floors were finished.

Weeks before the grand opening, every seat had been reserved. Twelve hours before the curtain rose, it was discovered that the stage could not be seen from the second row in the gallery. Work crews were called in, and the iron columns supporting the gallery were taken out, cut down eight inches and replaced, without cracking the ceiling plaster—a major engineering feat for the time.

On opening day, the excitement in town was not due to anticipation about the evening's performance but rather about an event that had taken place in the early morning. On the nineteenth, an attempt to rob a Leadville barber resulted in the barber killing one robber and wounding the other. The police arrested the thief, Patrick Stewart, and took him to jail. The next morning, citizens demanded that he be hanged. Officers told the marchers to return home or be arrested—this angered the marchers. Leadville had a reputation of letting thieves go with minor fines.

That night, a mob of masked men abducted a jail guard, threatening to kill him and his family if he did not help them. He told his colleagues to release the prisoner. The officers threw down their weapons, and the men stormed the jail, noticing that Stewart was not in a cell. Instead, he and Frodsham, another prisoner, were playing poker with the guards. The enraged mob took both Stewart and Frodsham.

The mob marched the prisoners along Harrison Avenue to a building under construction for Charles Boettcher's hardware store, directly across from the Tabor Opera House. The two were hanged from the rafters, with more than two thousand citizens witnessing the hanging of Edward Frodsham and Patrick Stewart.

When the bodies were cut down, a note was attached to Stewart's body that said:

> *To all you bonko steers, footpads and alike let this be your fate we are four hundred strong, The Vigilante Committee.*

As they say, the show must go on, and November 20, 1879, the Tabor Opera House officially opened to a packed house. The evening's performances were *Who's Who* and *A Serious Family*.

A few weeks later, Langrishe hired T.C. Howard to run the business department of the opera house. Howard acted with the stock company and was a familiar fixture in the early theaters in Leadville; Howard then hired Lou C. Leonard as treasurer to be in charge of the box office.

Phosa McAllister was the first leading lady; she played tragedy as well as comedy. Phosa stayed for almost two years, signing on with Langrishe, Knowles and Sullivan. When it was time to move on, many fellow actors joined her traveling troupe. She was given a large send-off at the Chestnut Street Theater, where she made more than $200 to start out on her own. She was replaced by Fannie Louise Buckingham.

Phosa was very successful traveling with her troupe before returning to the opera house in March 1882. Leadville packed the house. Many of the actors with the troupe were excited to see old friends. She returned again in February 1884 and was greeted by enthusiastic crowds. This was her last visit before gaining notoriety on New York and Chicago stages. Phosa died in 1909.

Reverend Mackey, the Episcopal minister, held services here twice on Sundays. On February 27, 1880, the crowd was so large there were more than two hundred people standing in the aisles. Although Reverend Mackey was preaching from his own church pulpit by 1881, the opera house continued to be used for other church services and functions.

Leadville did not have a law forbidding performances on Sunday, but it was frowned upon. The city council debated an ordinance closing all businesses on Sunday; however, the entertainment industry supporters prevailed. In 1879, there was a law that prevented an establishment from serving liquor on Sunday, but many of the saloon owners ignored it; Bush was one. He was arrested on September 1879 and fined fifty dollars.

On January 6, 1880, the Hibernian Society planned a meeting to discuss the famine in Ireland, and the opera house was chosen to hold a gathering of this size. The building's size also contributed to it being chosen for the funerals of Charles Vivian and Texas Jack—it was fitting that their funerals were held on a stage.

In February 1880, the stock company needed a leading man to play opposite Phosa McAllister. Langrishe was having respiratory difficulties and was confined to bed. Frank Roche was brought in to take over the leading male role. Roche had never performed here but was known by his reputation. It was standing room only when he played the lead in *Ingomar, the Barbarian*.

The miners went on strike in 1880. They were denied a pay raise, and they walked off the job, leaving the mines to fill with water. The smelter workers joined the strike. Stores closed and banks refused to renew loans. People were looking for a way to end the strike. Threats to burn the city were heard on every street.

The mine owners announced that unless adequate protection was given to the mines, they would close them and leave Leadville. W.L. Cooper, a merchant, went to Carlyle Davis, *Herald Democrat* editor, and said, "Davis, you can stop this strike and save Leadville!" Davis liked the idea, so he went to the businesses, calling for it to unite and end the strike.

A meeting was scheduled at Hallock's Hall, but the room was too small, so Davis moved it to the opera house. They formed the Committee of Safety, and Davis was chosen as chairman. The committee signed a charter promising to protect life and property in and around Leadville. The members wrote to Governor Pitkin, stating that the mayor and the police and sheriff departments sympathized with the strikers; therefore, they could not depend on them to protect life or property. They requested he declare martial law. The governor asked the committee to exhaust every resource first, so the committee formed seven companies of one hundred men for guard duty; the fire departments were also brought in to assist.

Harrison Avenue filled with eight thousand striking miners on one side, with the committee's guards on the other. At about noon, Davis and Lieutenant Governor Tabor stood on the balcony of the opera house and read the proclamation set forth by the Committee of Safety. It stated that they would do whatever necessary to protect life and property, and if the mine owners would not yield to demands, they would bring in men to replace the striking miners.

Davis said, "I did not expect to leave the balcony alive. I had a feeling akin to disappointment that the reading of the proclamation was not interrupted with a rifle ball." The crowd left the street safely, and the next day, the committee again appealed to the governor and the request was granted. Governor Pitkin issued a proclamation on June 18, 1880, saying,

"Leadville is in a state of siege. Five Companies of the State Militia have been sent to Leadville."

Martial law meant that no more than two men could gather in one place at any time. Captain Rose ordered all saloons and any place that served liquor closed. Although performances had been scheduled, the stage of the opera house went dark. Military headquarters was set up at the opera house, and no one was granted admittance. Martial law was lifted on June 22, 1880.

Leadville again came under martial law in 1896, and the opera house became the meeting place for negotiations. When the union miners went on strike, several of the mine owners employed scabs and fired the union workers rather than give into their demands. On September 20, 1896, the Coronado Mine was dynamited, destroying the mine. Several miners and one fireman were killed (the fireman was shot while trying to put out the fire). The men gathered at the opera house to discuss the tragedy and a resolution; however, martial law was ordered, and the military arrived the following day. The opera house hosted talks a week later to try to end the strikes; more than one thousand union miners attended.

"Texas Jack" Omohundro and his wife, Madame Josephine Morlacchi, arrived in the spring of 1880. Josephine had just finished an engagement in Denver and was looking forward to Leadville. T.C. Howard and Jack Langrishe were excited to book Josephine at the Tabor Opera House; she performed for six nights in *The French Spy* and *My Pretty Jane*.

Sullivan and Howard had been talking about forming an independent troupe to put on *The Black Crook*. They were both familiar with the production in New York. Josephine was excited to perform in the great play and signed on to be a part of the show. It is not known whether it was Tabor, Bush or Langrishe, but it was ultimately decided that *The Black Crook* was not a good fit for the opera house.

In April 1880, Howard and Sullivan approached the Grand Central Theater, which was happy to have the play there. Josephine opened a studio on the third floor and taught ballet while she was practicing for the performance.

Texas Jack wanted to do some prospecting, certain that he would strike it rich. He went prospecting by day and at night was a guard in the Tabor Light Cavalry. While on duty in the cold night air, he caught pneumonia; already suffering from consumption, he could not fight off the new illness. He died on June 28, 1880, at the residence of Charlie Howard, with Josephine by his side.

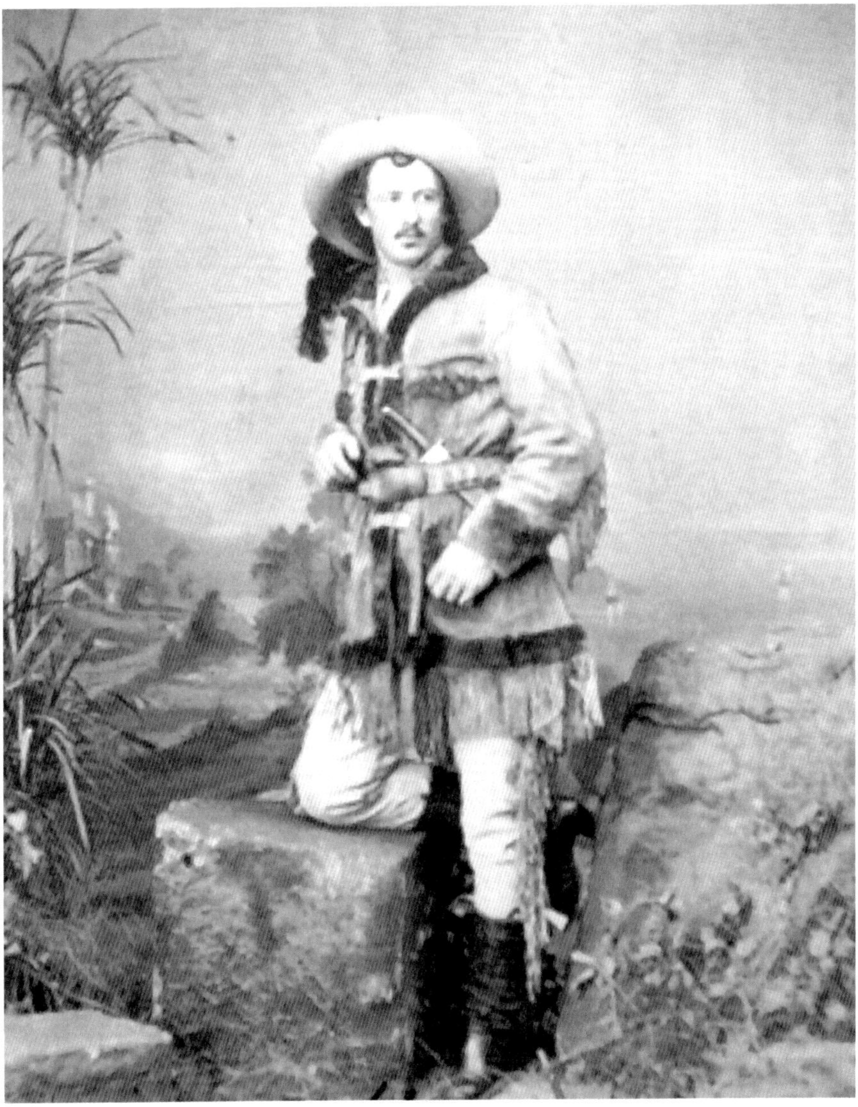

John Baker Omohundro "Texas Jack."

The funeral at the opera house was a grand military service, with every organization in Leadville participating, along with hundreds of actors. The coffin was elegant, with a silver plate inscribed, "John B. Omohundro—Aged 30 Years." A member of the Pickett Light Cavalry painted a wooden headstone with a picture of his favorite horse's head and a gun belt with two guns.

Josephine fainted during the ceremony and was unable to get out of the coach at the cemetery to go to her husband's final resting place. Texas Jack had squandered their money in the pursuit of a larger fortune. Josephine was left penniless; her estate in Lowell, Massachusetts, and her jewelry were auctioned off to pay his debts.

A benefit performance of *The French Spy* was given on July 10 by Grand Central's actors, including Howard and Sullivan. Another was given at the Tabor Opera House on August 5 by Buffalo Bill and his family to help Josephine with the costs of returning home. She left Leadville a few weeks later to live with her sister in Massachusetts, where she remained until her death on July 23, 1886.

Buffalo Bill returned to Leadville in September 1908, bringing the Wild West & Congress of Rough Riders for its first performance after touring Europe. He arranged a memorial service for his friend, Texas Jack, with one hundred members of the show. The Wild West Band played at the grave site, while many came to pay their last respects: Buffalo Bill and John Burke, as well as several soldiers, scouts, cowboys and Rough Riders. In attendance were several Native American chiefs and tribal members who knew Jack from prior skirmishes. Buffalo Bill made arrangements to have a permanent granite marker replace the worn wooden headstone.

Former president Ulysses Grant was invited to Leadville by the Grand Army of the Republic. Grant arrived in July 1880 on one of the first railroad trains to enter Leadville. He was scheduled to attend a performance of *Our Boarding House* at the Tabor Opera House, but the train was late and the play had already begun. The actors stopped performing, and the orchestra played "Hail to the Chief."

A grand ball was held at the City Hall in Grant's honor during his five-day visit. After the ball, Grant retired to his rooms at the Clarendon Hotel; some of his party, including Tabor, went in search of more local entertainment.

At the Pioneer Saloon on State Street, some miners were staging a bet, claiming to have caught a badger, which they were holding in a barrel, and he was going to fight Bad Pete, a bulldog who belonged to the owner of the Board of Trade Saloon known to "bar-hop" for his dish of warm beer.

Bets were taken; odds were in favor of the badger, which was making a racket in the back of the bar, causing Bad Pete to growl and lunge at the barrel. The miners put stovepipes on their legs for protection and shoved the dog in the barrel. Such a racket ensued. The gentlemen had no sooner placed their bets when Leadville's marshal arrived, saw what was happening and placed everyone under arrest. He informed them that they would be seen by a judge later in the week. They protested, saying that they had to leave with Grant in the morning.

The marshal offered to hold the trial immediately, if they agreed. A judge was secured and the courthouse opened, and proceedings lasted all night; every miner took the stand and blamed Grant's men for the fight. The men were impatient, not wanting to miss the train. The judge declared them guilty. He demanded that they bring in the dead badger so that the men could see the terrible destruction they had caused. The barrel was opened to reveal a chain and a chamber pot that rolled out on the floor.

It took a full two minutes before things calmed down, and the men realized there never was a badger. It was all a hoax. The judge then read from a card:

> *Advice:*
> *Don't wrestle in the mud with pigs;*
> *Don't get into a pissing match with a skunk;*
> *Don't play leapfrog with a unicorn;*
> *Don't get in the middle of a badger fight;*
> *And finally, don't muck with Leadville.*

The men rushed to meet their group and the departing train. The marshal and the miners split the bets. This whole event was repeated many times on unsuspecting visitors; it was later turned into a play and performed for many years.

Early in 1881, the stage belonged to Fannie Louise Buckingham and her gray horse, James Melville. She packed the house every matinee and evening. Fannie was also famous for playing the male lead in *Mazzepa* and *Dick Turpin*—one of the few women in the United States to play a male role. *Mazzepa* is based on Ivan Stepanovich Mazzepa's life.

This was the year of female leading actresses. Fannie Buckingham was followed by Minnie Palmer, Kate Claxton, Maude Granger, Charlotte Thompson and Emily Soldene. Kate Claxton came to Leadville in the spring for *Two Orphans*. It was not a standing room–only performance, despite its great success in other towns. Her performance in *Double Marriage* was one the crowd and Leadville critics loved best, saying that she made her character of Gilberto a most attractive woman.

Maude Granger played in Leadville for five days beginning April 25. Leadville was excited about the much-anticipated performance; all tickets had sold out before she even arrived. Granger traveled with a small supporting cast that played the leading characters in *Camille*, *Frou Frou*, *Forbidden Fruit* and *Lady of Lyons*. They were supported by Langrishe's troupe for the minor roles.

In her role in *Camille*, Maude gave one of the best performances seen thus far in Leadville. Reviews said that the portrayal was "perfection." The leading man was Ogden Stevens, playing Armand; reviewers said that he was a very capable actor and gave a good performance. The next night, in *Forbidden Fruit*, Jack Langrishe replaced Stevens as the leading man.

A few weeks later, on May 20, Charlotte Thompson and Will Sheridan performed *Camille*, sparking a debate by theatergoers over who presented a better Camille. Thompson performed in a more traditional style, while Granger adapted it to her highly dramatic style. Everyone agreed that Will Sheridan's Armand was much stronger than Ogden Stevens's.

The opera house was considered the safest and most respectable amusement in town, a place where you could take your wife. On June 14, 1881, it was touched by what was thought to only affect the gaudy theaters of State Street. A woman, dressed in black, with a veil covering her face, gave her money to the ticket taker because the performance *Othello* had begun. Soon she exited the auditorium, followed by a gentleman; a few people gathered to see if a real-life tragedy was unfolding. The woman aimed a small handgun at the man. He grabbed her hand and whispered, "For god's sake, Mattie, let's not make a scene." He pulled her from the building, and they got in a hack and disappeared. They were never identified, but speculation said that the Tabor Opera House was a good place to take not only the wife but the mistress as well.

In 1881, Tabor hired J.H. Cragg to manage the opera house and bring in the best traveling companies. This became easier in 1884 when Tabor hired Peter McCourt (Baby Doe's brother) to manage the Tabor Grand Opera House in Denver. McCourt formed the Colorado Circuit (also known as the Tabor Circuit), which booked traveling theatricals and opera companies in Colorado theaters and opera houses. When the railroad was completed through the Colorado Rockies, he added Utah cities. Southern Wyoming towns were added earlier. All circuit towns were on a railroad line, splitting travel costs among many locations. Two associates in New York contracted with the troupes and arranged the theater dates.

McCourt announced the formation of the Silver Circuit on March 6, 1888; however, the inauguration was on July 1, 1889, when the Salida, Pueblo and Aspen opera houses were completed. The circuit included thirteen stops: Denver; Leadville; Aspen; Salida; Colorado Springs, Pueblo and Trinidad in Colorado; Salt Lake City, Provo, Ogden and Park City in Utah; and Evanston and Rawlins in Wyoming. The list was updated annually, when ownership changed or a theater was lost due to fire.

Troupes traveled from the East, playing one show two to three nights in each town. Often they played at the Tabor Opera House, headed west and returned on their way east. Railroads jumped at the opportunity to promote rail travel by advertising towns along the circuit as "good show towns." They also catered to the troupes by pulling an extra car to carry their scenes and costumes.

When Tabor lost both opera houses, McCourt went in business for himself, booking shows for a small percentage. The Tabor Opera House stayed on the circuit through Weston's ownership and, for many years, through the Elks' ownership. Later, moving pictures became popular, and fewer troops were traveling, so they were booked on the same circuit. Peter McCourt died in Denver on April 5, 1929, the Silver Circuit passing with him.

Oscar Wilde came to America on January 3, 1882, and embarked on a year-long tour. He arrived in Leadville on April 13. The large crowd waiting in the lobby of the Clarendon Hotel, however, didn't get to see him because he slipped in through the ladies' entrance and went to his room. He requested a doctor because he was having trouble breathing. The doctor said that it was due to the elevation and that rest was the best thing. After that, Wilde was interviewed by a reporter from the *Herald*; he lay on the couch, saying that he was too sick to rise.

He said he enjoyed the train ride. He went up to the engine and had a long conversation with the engineer, who was delighted to find that Wilde was an Irishman. He saw bluebirds along the way and felt that they were almost as pretty as kingfishers. The reporter quoted Wilde as saying, "I love to travel and meet the best of men and look at the best and most beautiful women, so when I die I will leave behind a name that will be handed down posterity as a lover of Beautiful."

Wilde was late arriving that night at the Tabor Opera House, and the patrons were getting restless. When he took the stage, he came in front of the curtain and said, "I give myself to Leadville." Local lore says that a stagehand, arranging a chair, accidently hit the hand-painted drop curtain, and Wilde fell into the orchestra pit.

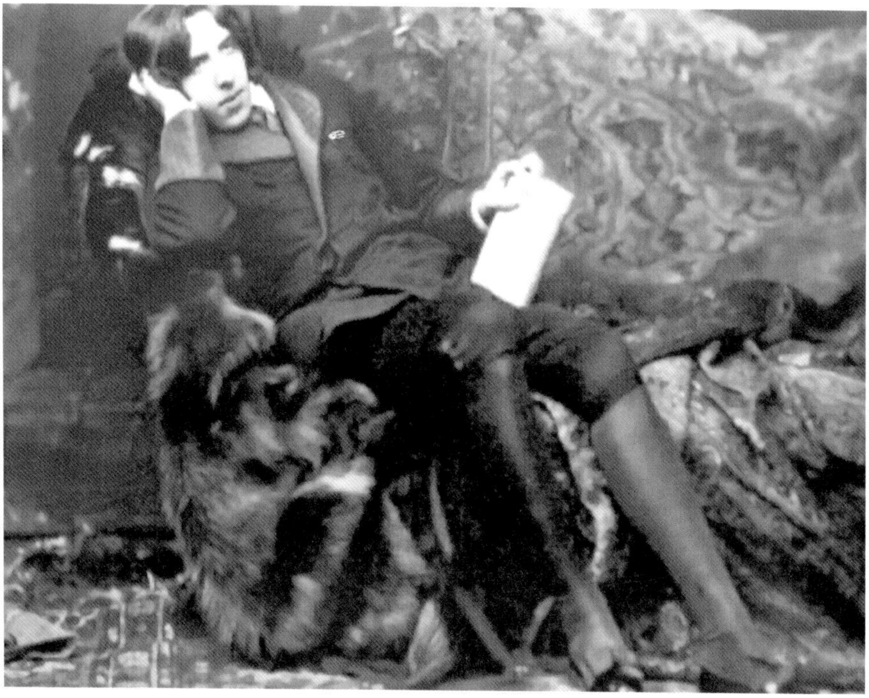

Oscar Wilde.

He wore a dark velvet suit with a cutaway coat, the satin lining decorated with storks and ferns. At his neck was a Byron collar and flossy white neckerchief. A single cluster of diamonds adorned his chest. Knee-breeches, low shoes and black stockings completed his attire. Wilde's hair was straight, parted in the middle, and fell over his shoulders.

The miners expressed quite a reaction to his attire. Some of the things said on the street included "Sissy boy"; "His suit was the prettiest purple, but it was more suited to a woman's gown than a man's suit"; "His pants were designed for a boy"; and "Who would wear short pants and low shoes when the snow would cover them?"

Wilde lectured for an hour on the "Ethics of Art." During his lecture, Wilde read passages from the autobiography of Benevento Cellini. Someone asked him why he didn't bring Cellini with him, to which he replied that the man was dead. Someone shouted, "Who shot him?"

After the lecture, Wilde and his agent, Richard D'Oyly Carte, were taken on a tour and dinner down in the Matchless Mine; he wore a protective suit

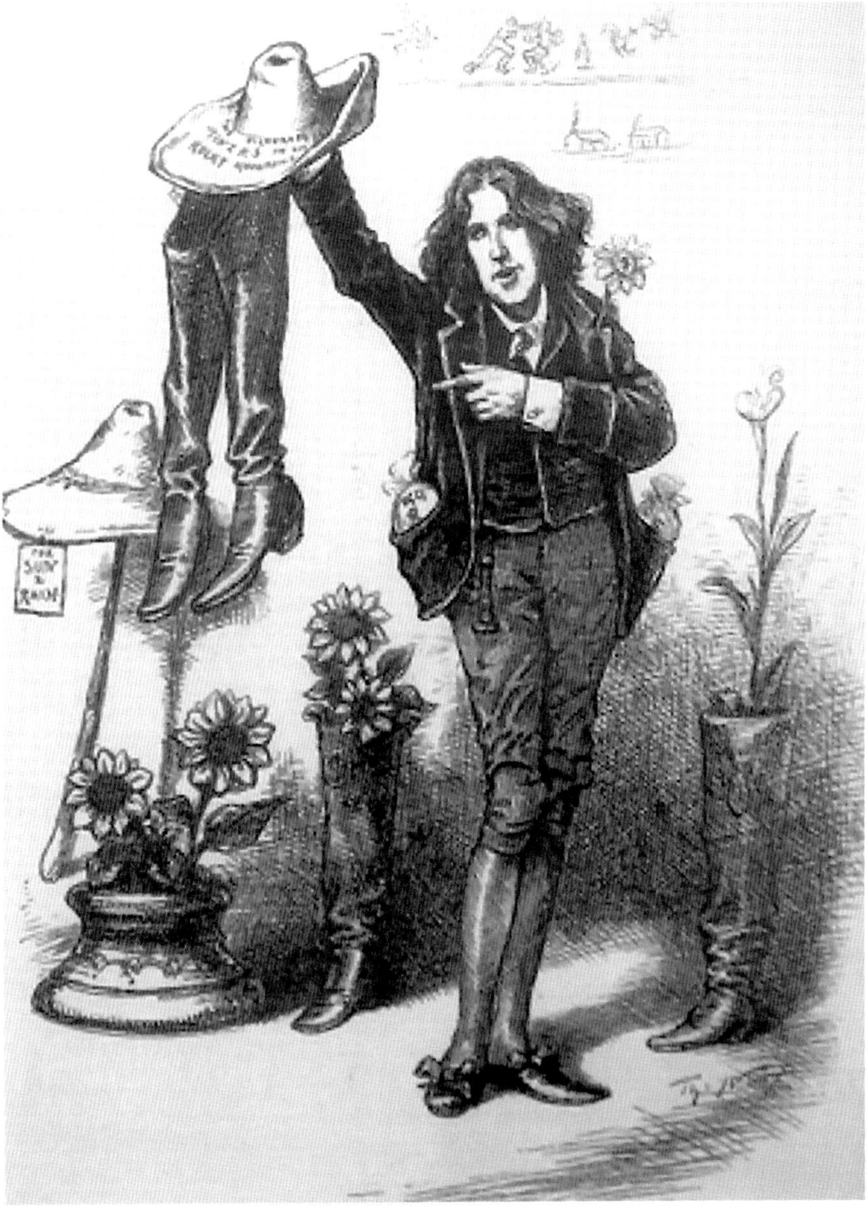

Depiction of Oscar Wilde during his trip west.

given to him by Horace Tabor. He said, "The first course was whiskey, the second course whiskey, and the third course the same; my kind of meal." Then Wilde was handed a silver drill and given the honor of opening a new lode, named "Oscar." He was given the drill as a souvenir, although he said that he wished he had gotten a share of the lode. It is interesting that he opened a silver vein because he said, "When I was at Leadville and reflected on all the shinning silver I saw coming from the mines, to be made into ugly dollars, it made me sad. The gold gates at Florence are as beautiful today as when Michelangelo saw them."

Next, several miners took him to Pap Wyman's Saloon to try to drink him under the table. However, Oscar Wilde was the last man standing. Much later, local miners reflected on the event, saying, "Wilde could drink all night and then carry two of us home."

Wilde noted the sign over the piano at Pap's that said, "Don't shoot the pianist; he is doing the best he can." He said that it was the most rational method of art criticism he had seen and that Leadville must go through a lot of pianists.

When he returned to England and wrote about his tour, he said two men had been hanged before he went on stage. It is believed that he was referring to the opening night of the opera house and not to a hanging prior to his theater engagement. Wilde also said that before coming to Leadville, he was told, "If I went there they would be sure to shoot me or my traveling manager. I said nothing they could do to my traveling manager would intimidate me. I found the miners very charming and not rough at all." Oscar Wilde's visit to Leadville was the talk of the town for many months.

In August 1882, the opera house was closed for renovations because of problems with the acoustics and ventilation. The frescoed ceiling was removed, and the roof was raised three inches. Eighty-six jack screws and iron plates were placed to bridge the roof and hold the new duck-canvas ceiling. Columns were added for support, and additional windows were cut in the south wall for ventilation. Finally, several seats were removed to allow for more space between patrons; state-of-the-art scene-shifting equipment was also added to the stage.

In February 1883, J. Cragg purchased the first movie projector, an oxy-hydrogen Stereopticon with a double lantern, along with 1,200 pictures of Europe and America. Patrons were excited to see this newest technology.

The Mestayer's Company performed at the opera house on April 16 in *Tourist in a Pullman Palace Car*. The entire performance was performed inside a Pullman car on the stage; it was a comedy farce about a tourist on his way to California. The troupe traveled by train, bringing all the sets, the scenes and the Pullman car.

Kate Castleton made her first appearance at the opera house in April in *Rice's Surprise Party*. Little is known of how the play was received; however, she returned several times over the next few years to sold-out crowds. On May 18, 1887, Kate and her company were on their way to Leadville, for the sold-out show *Crazy Patch* when the Rio Grande Railroad derailed outside of Salida. Grace Leslie, an actress, was killed. Kate and the rest of the cast were too upset to perform any of the scheduled nights.

Luckily, Kate's husband and manager, Harry Phillips, was able to find quiet lodging for them to rest and heal. He also made arrangements to send Grace Leslie's body east for burial.

Kate Castleton returned in March 1888. When it was announced that she would play in Leadville, she added that "as long as none of her crew fell victim to our mountain railroads, she would be here." Unfortunately, the train was delayed several days due to blizzards in Kansas. The cast couldn't obtain a sleeping car, and they missed the performances in Pueblo and Colorado Springs. When they finally arrived, they had time to grab only a few hours of sleep before going on stage.

A large, eager crowd waited to see them perform in *Crazy Patch*. The audience said that it was worth the wait. In her company was the famous vaudeville actor Edwin "Eddie" Foy. He was no stranger to Leadville, having held the lead at the Comique Theater when it first opened.

In April 1889, Kate came back to an excited crowd at the opera house, playing in *A Paper Doll*. It was well received, playing to an almost full house. *The Dazzler*, an incredibly successful play, played at the opera house in October 1891, again with Kate Castleton in the lead.

Over the years, the audience was treated to some unusual props and performances. On August 22, 1884, the Madison Square Theater Company performed *The Rajah* with a real stream of running water across the stage. The Wallick Company stunned audiences in *The Bandit King* when the players acted out a duel between two men on horseback, fighting with Bowie knifes. On June 6, 1890, *Pine Meadow* included a herd of sheep on the stage.

On May 23, 1887, William Cameron Coup and P.T. Barnum's circus came to the opera house. The circus traveled on its own train, even though the troupe was smaller than the tent circus. The audiences cheered as they watched a pony named Nick impersonating a rocking horse. Nick also performed in a skit in which he acted as a student, with the other students acting as clowns.

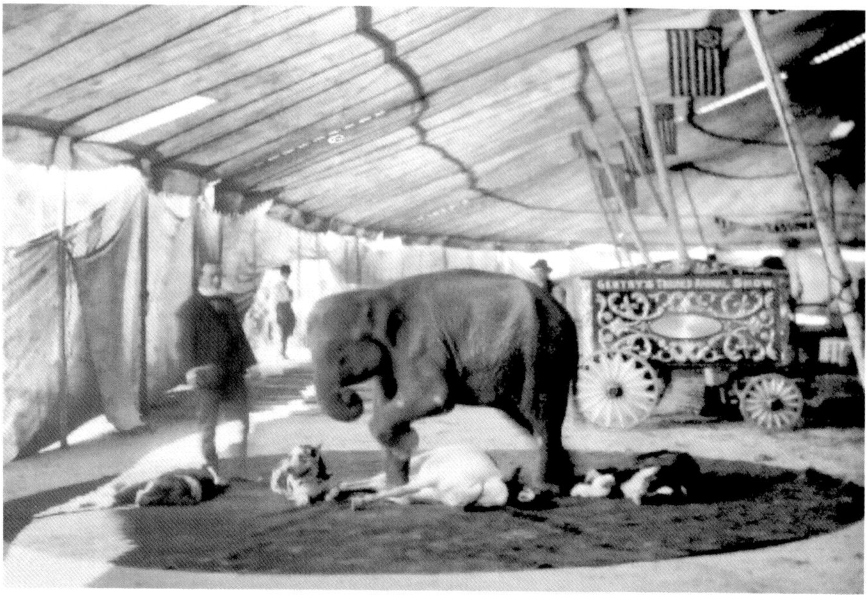

Circus act in about 1880.

The show included a band of dogs, performing various tricks; the Elliot's Trick Unicycle Riders, ranging from six to forty years old; and six-year-old "Little Dot," who amazed the audience with her skill on the one-wheeled bike, performing a series of balancing and jumps. Another highlight was Toby the elephant performing a military march.

In the grand finale, horses lined up on the stage, while another horse, with a cannon strapped to his back, shot at the line of horses; after each shot, one dropped to the floor and played dead. The audience was delighted.

Madame Modjeska was accompanied by Maurice Barrymore, and the review noted that he was faultless. Overall, reviews for the company were favorable. Mrs. Barrows, another actress, was given rave reviews. According to the *Leadville Evening Chronicle*, the performances were poorly attended after the first night.

When Maurice Barrymore left Leadville, a young lady followed him to Denver, confessing her undying love. He rejected her, saying that he was married with two children. She returned home and turned her attentions to another young man. It is unusual that Maurice turned away this young lady's affection, as he was known to have had many affairs over the years. One, with Helena Modjeska herself, continued for many years.

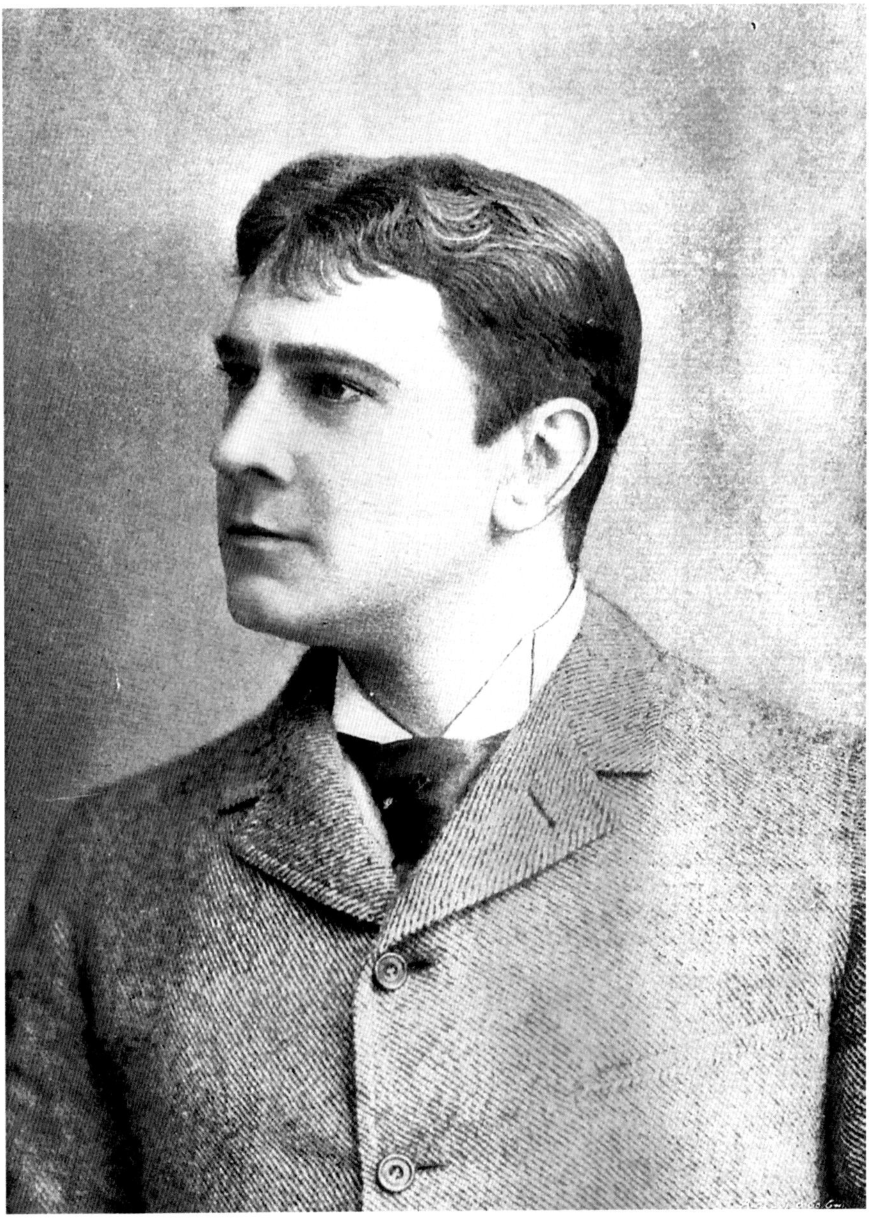

Maurice Barrymore. *From* The Marie Burroughs Art Portfolio of Stage Celebrities *(A.N. Marquis and Company, 1894).*

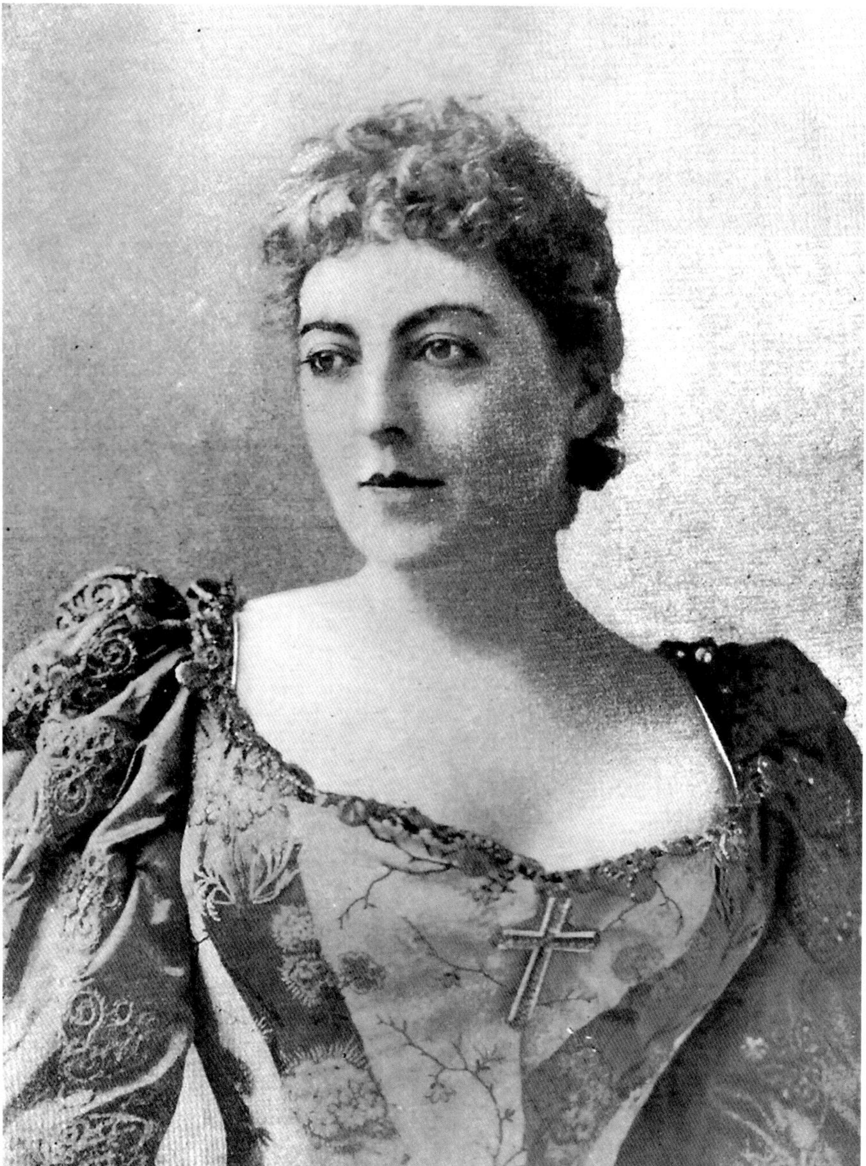

Georgina Drew, wife of Maurice Barrymore. *From* The Marie Burroughs Art Portfolio of Stage Celebrities *(A.N. Marquis and Company, 1894).*

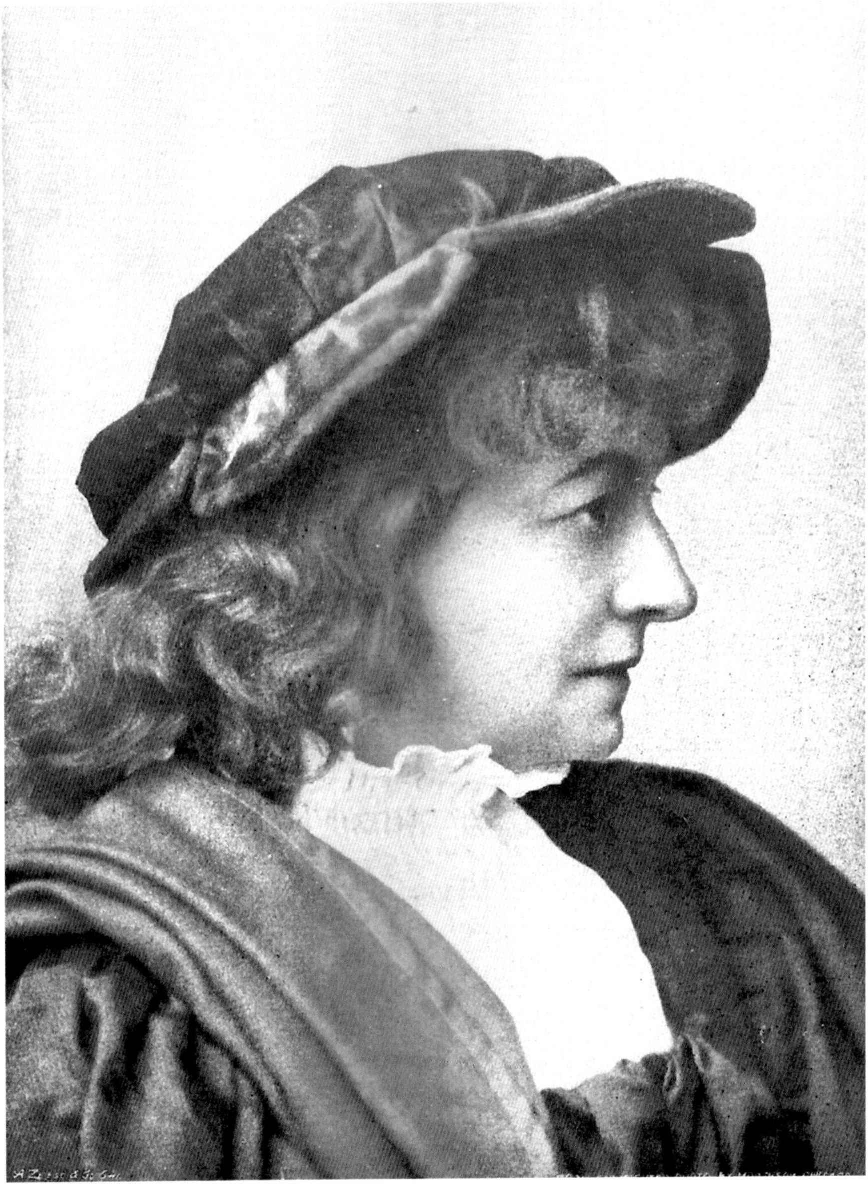

Helen Modjeska. *From* The Marie Burroughs Art Portfolio of Stage Celebrities *(A.N. Marquis and Company, 1894).*

Modjeska returned to the opera house in July 1889 in *Adrienne le Couvreur* and *As You Like It*. The reviews called her "brilliant" and "truly magnificent" and the work itself "the most exquisite play Leadville had seen."

Madame was interviewed on the morning of July 18 and was asked for her thoughts on Leadville and Colorado. She stated, "Colorado is beautiful. I can never get enough of its scenery." About Leadville, she said, "Your people are not strange to me. Although you live high, you are the most enthusiastic people in the world." She also talked about how excited she was about her upcoming outing. She and her husband, Count Bozentia, along with other cast members, had planned a horseback ride to Evergreen Lakes. The party rode down Leadville's famous boulevard to Evergreen Lakes and Soda Springs. They spent the afternoon at the resort and enjoyed dinner at the Mount Massive Hotel, returning for the evening's performance.

In 1892, Maurice Barrymore's wife, Georgina, visited Leadville. It is not known whether her husband accompanied her, as she was traveling with Charles Frohman's Comedian Company. She played a small part in *Mr. Wilkinson's Widow*, here for one night; the reviews indicated that it was well received. Georgina Barrymore was born Georgiana Drew, and she is the great-grandmother of actress Drew Blythe Barrymore. Maurice Barrymore, born Herbert Arthur Chamberlayne Blythe, was her great-grandfather.

In February 1887, the Hebrew Ladies' Benevolent Association planned its eighth annual Purim Ball. It was usually held at the City Hall, but the club decided that it was too small and moved it to the Tabor Opera House. The opera house did not have a large hall or ballroom. The floor sloped toward the stage, and the theater seats were bolted to the floor.

The date for the ball was moved from March to April in order to create a dance floor. A large platform was constructed that joined the stage and extended out, covering the opera chairs. The platform was thirty-five by sixty-five feet, with wings on each side measuring fifteen by thirty feet. Professor Zilm's thirteen-piece orchestra sat on a raised platform in the gallery. Over center stage hung a large Star of David decorated in red, white and blue. No part of the building was bare—additional flags, banners and bunting hung everywhere. This masquerade ball was considered one of the most elegant ever held in Leadville.

The opera house was packed on April 7, 1888, to see *The Gypsy Barron*, presented by the Conried Opera Company. Although the company was reputable and the show considered a "must see," many people gathered to see the electric lights more than the performance. Charles Boettcher, owner of Boettcher's Leadville Electric Light Company, had donated the lights used in the second act. They gave the prop ruins on the stage a more realistic effect. Although some buildings already had electric lights, they were still a big hit.

Robert Downing played in *The Gladiator* on May 30, and the crowd loved it. Newspapers reported that "there has never been a grander reception given to a play at the Opera House. Joseph Mack, the company manager, spent a great deal of money to change the scene every time the curtain was raised. When the curtain opened, there was a large model of the Coliseum on stage." The crowd called Downing back seven times for curtain calls; he was definitely a Leadville favorite.

In June, H.A.W. Tabor offered to sell the opera house to A.V. Hunter, George Trimble and August Meyer. The option remained open until July 1. However, no reply was received. Also, that month, the opera house site was considered as a possible location for the new post office.

There must have been an incident during the engagement of the Dockstander's Minstrels in July. Two days after they left, the manager, J.H. Cragg, posted a sign on the stage:

No Kicking!
There is only one way to get along pleasantly on this stage, and that is to be pleasant.
When it comes to kicking we will be right there.
No strangers allowed behind the scenes except by permission of the manager.
No loud talking, swearing or noise of any kind will be allowed.
We will do anything to please anyone, but of course some people come here who think they have played in larger finer houses. It is a mistake.
It is an not easy thing for us, at a moment's notice, to move any dressing room, furnish all with grand pianos, electric lights, hot and cold running water, easy chairs, etc.
People who are never used to anything in their lives always kick the most. They are what I call common people.
Manager J.H. Cragg

There was a packed house on May 29, 1889, for Reilly & Wood's *New Big Show*. The headline act was the Vaidis Sisters, "Queens of the Trapeze." The twins had been performing since they were little girls and had gained the reputation as the best women on the trapeze by the time they ventured to Leadville. They had fans from when they performed at the Bella Union Theater in Deadwood; many Leadville miners also spent

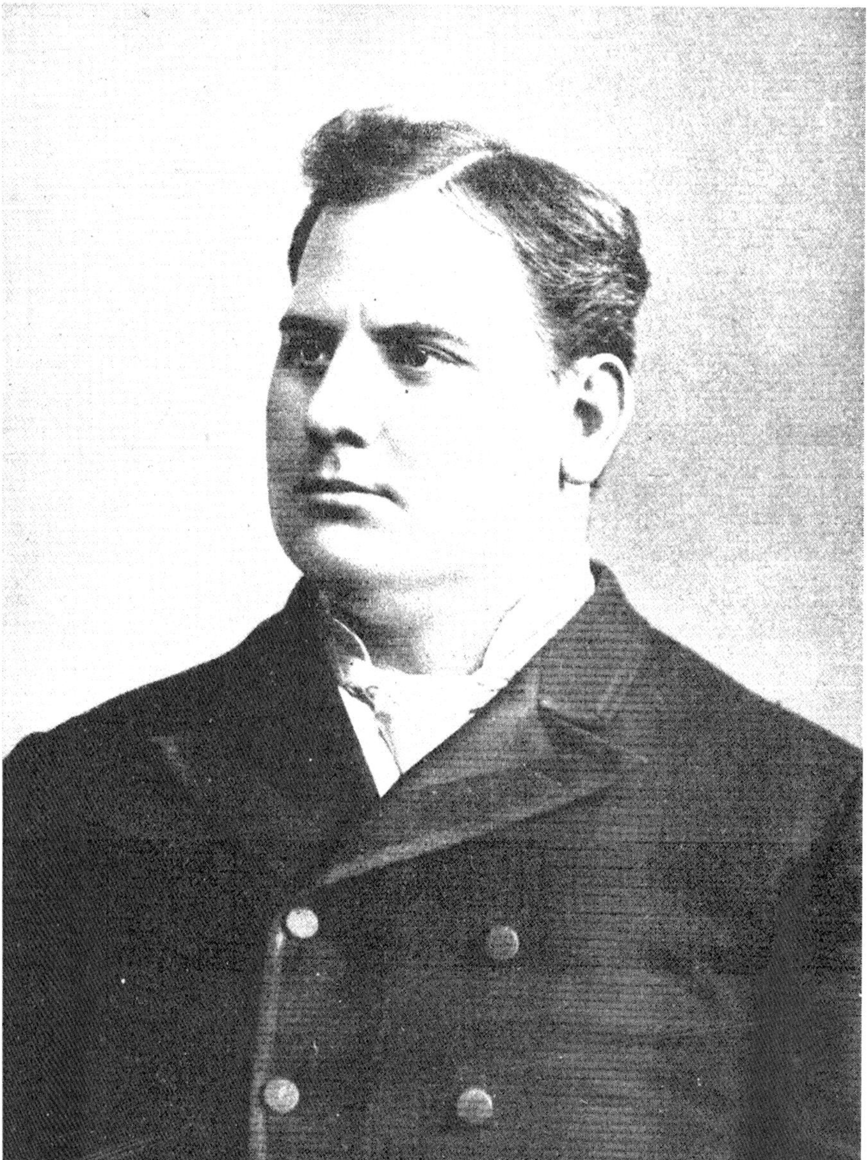

Robert Downing. *From* The Marie Burroughs Art Portfolio of Stage Celebrities *(A.N. Marquis and Company, 1894).*

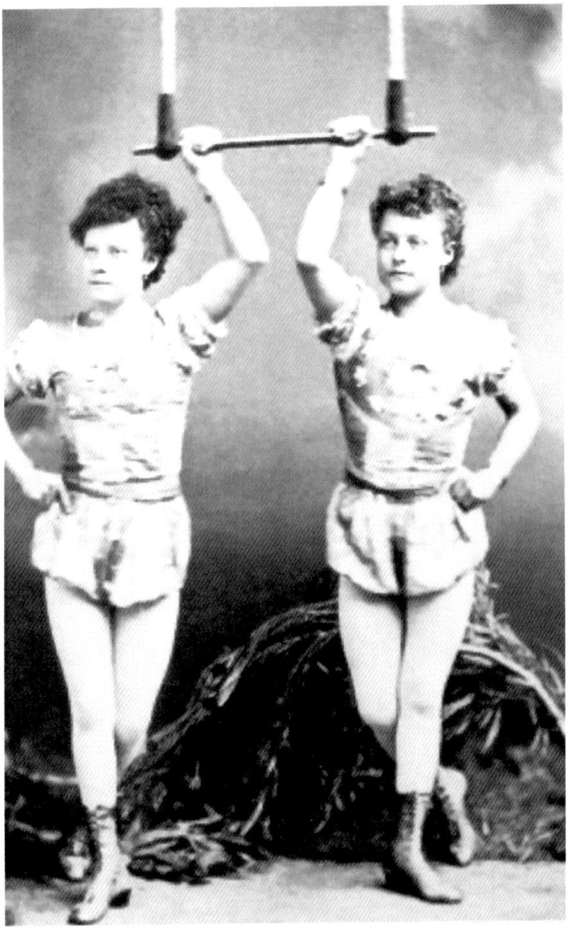

The Vaidis Sisters, "Queens of the Trapeze."

time in Deadwood. The sisters did not disappoint the audience. They performed many death-defying feats on a revolving double trapeze, high above the audience.

On July 15, 1890, extra chairs were added to accommodate the crowd that came to see former Leadville actor Bobby Gaylor. Even those who purchased a standing room–only ticket felt lucky to have gotten in. Bobby first appeared in the fourth act, and the audience leaped to its feet, yelling and waving programs. He gave the crowd one of his signature turns, delighting the people even more. Gaylor was involved in a sparring match on the stage, and the audience stood and cheered during the event. After the show, they called Bobby back for four curtain calls. Finally, he spoke about how excited

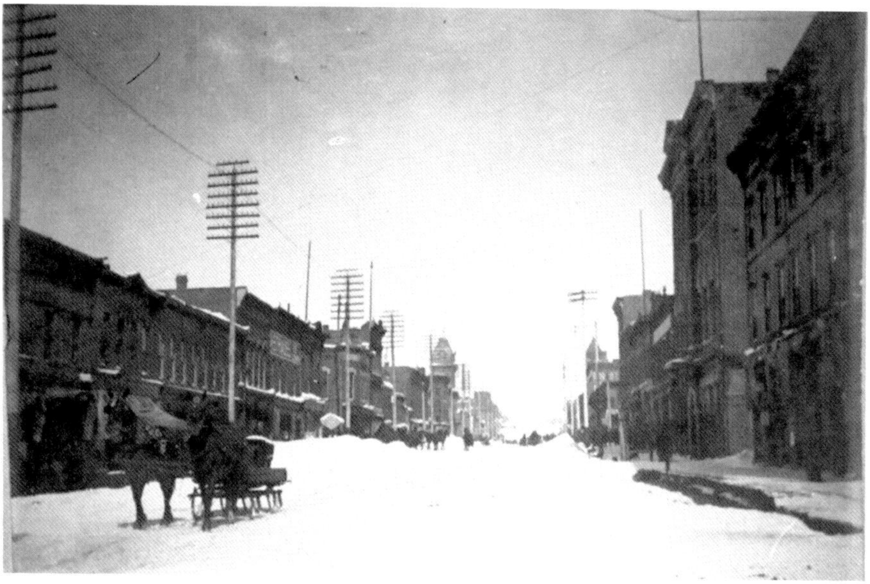

Harrison Avenue. On the extreme right is the Clarendon Hotel, and the Tabor Opera House is next to it. In the middle of the block, the building on the left, with the dome, is the court house. *Courtesy of the Colorado Mountain History Collection, Lake County Public Library.*

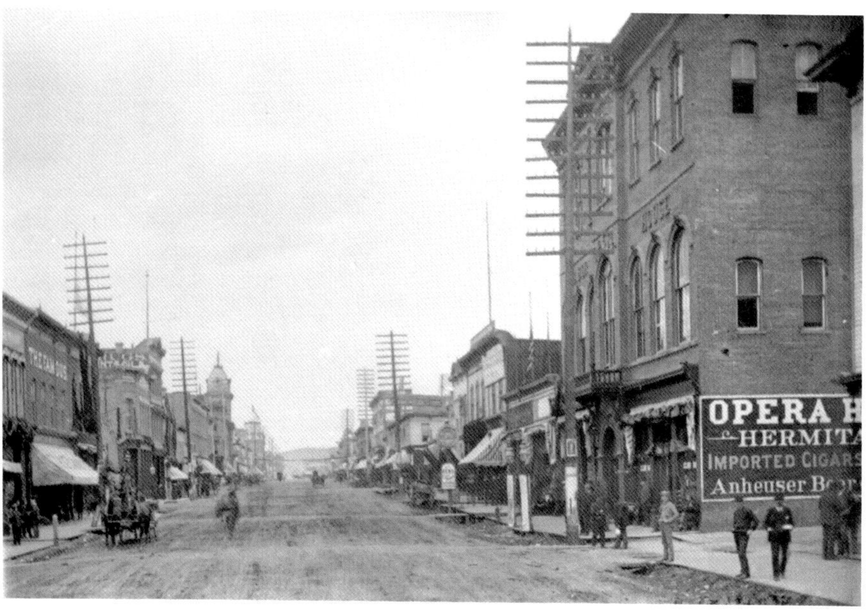

Tabor Opera House. *Courtesy of the Colorado Mountain History Collection, Lake County Public Library.*

he was to be back in Leadville. The company and Bobby played for three more nights; each night the crowd was just as enthusiastic as the first.

The Knowles troupe left in 1880, and Tabor hired F.T. Osgood to manage the theater. He stayed for almost two years before being replaced by James Cragg. Cragg managed operations until 1890 and then moved to Denver to work as the Silver Circuit secretary. The success of the opera house depended more on Cragg than Tabor. Cragg said that if one man liked a show, there was another who hated it.

Cragg closed the theater for part of July and August (so it could be updated) while he was in Denver learning his new duties. Mr. Burkay, an artist from the Tabor Grand Opera House, painted new scenery for the next season, as well as some of the much-needed interior scenes. Craftsmen updated the aging theater. Newspapers reported, "She has fallen behind some of the newer, modern theaters." Manager Cragg wrote to Tabor with the hope of completely remodeling the theater, but Tabor replied, "No, only the absolute necessary improvements would be made." Windows were added to the balcony to help with ventilation, exits were improved and another exit was added to the north side of the building.

Weston Opera House

On April 7, 1893, Judge Algernon S. Weston acquired the Tabor Opera House and held a warranty deed for $32,000, but the name was not changed until May 5, 1894. Weston was known as a man of reputation, a staunch supporter of the law and one of Leadville's leading residents. He arrived in Lake County in the 1860s and resided in Oro City. Elected in 1861, he was one of the first county commissioners. In 1871, he purchased a ranch eight miles from Leadville and studied law at night.

In 1872, Weston was admitted to the Colorado Territory Bar. He was the only lawyer in Lake County until 1877, defending some of Leadville's leading citizens, as well as some of its lowest. In 1879, he was elected judge and, in 1880, state senator. Weston was an investor in the Humboldt Mining and Smelting Company, making a small fortune off his investment. Weston and Tabor were friends during the early days. Weston served as a senator, while Tabor was lieutenant governor of Colorado. The two saw eye to eye on almost every issue except the 1881 silver resolution.

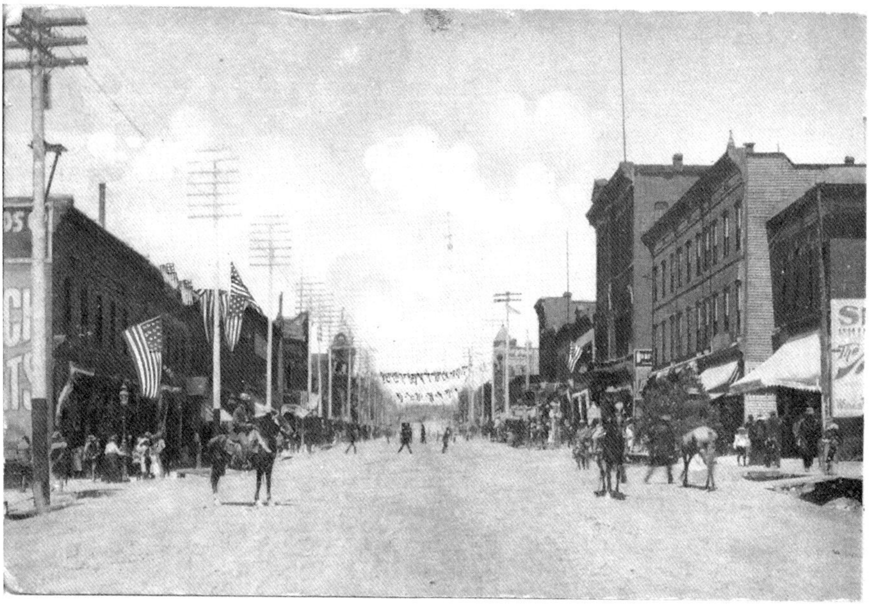

Postcard of Harrison Avenue showing the Weston Opera House. *Author's collection.*

Judge Weston died on March 30, 1897, leaving behind his second wife, Letitia, and several children. He bequeathed the opera house to Letitia, making her one of five women who owned theaters in the United States. Letitia took over the management and day-to-day operations, moving into the upstairs rooms that had once been the office of Mr. Tabor.

Magicians were a favorite of the theaters, always delighting and mystifying audiences. Professor Anton Zamloch, Austrian conjuror and exposer of spiritualism, was the first magician to take the stage at the Tabor Opera House, on November 20, 1880. Zamloch the Great was a big hit when he held a wire cage containing a live canary, advanced into the audience and, with an upward toss of his hand, made the cage and bird disappear. He kept audiences in good humor with his amazing and humorous deceptions. The press eagerly provided coverage for his appearances.

Every seat was filled on June 8, 1896. The crowd waited anxiously to see if the stories of the "boy hypnotist" were true. Professor Gunning, who looked like a young boy, took the stage and performed a few tricks. At the end of the show, he asked for a volunteer who would not be busy the next few days. Ralph Barr volunteered, and Gunning put Barr in a trance.

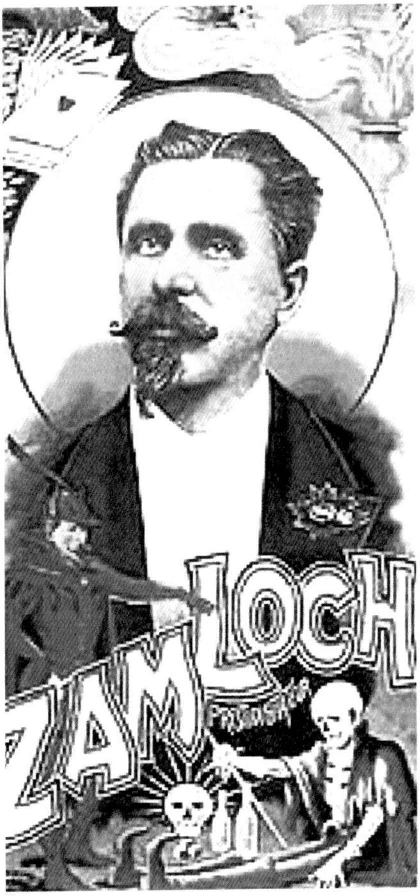

Poster of Zamloch the Great.

Men were assigned to guard Barr, and two days later, everyone wanted to see if he was still asleep. He was brought on stage on a stretcher, followed by the guards, who assured the audience that Barr had not stirred. The Professor woke Barr by rubbing his hands across his face. A doctor declared that Barr had lost eight pounds during his sleep.

On August 18, 1897, more than two thousand people lined Harrison Avenue to watch Alex J. McIvor-Tydall, a well-known spiritualist, clairvoyant and hypnotist, make his way to the opera house for the evening's performance. Earlier that day, a ribbon was hidden along Harrison Avenue, and Tydall promised to find it while blindfolded. He climbed in his carriage and led his horses down the avenue at a run. Stopping in front of Nowland's Bookstore, he reached in the awning and grabbed the ribbon. Tydall returned to the carriage, sped down the avenue and stopped in front of the opera house—all without removing his blindfold. The event brought roars of approval from the crowd.

Tydall stayed in Leadville for a few extra days, greeting visitors, answering questions and deciphering their deepest secrets. One morning, a well-known lady told him about her ring, one very precious to her. She believed that it had been stolen. She asked Tydall to identify the thief. After a few minutes, he said that he could see the ring in a section of pipe behind her sink. She rushed home and told her husband that they must remove the sink at once. The ring was found exactly where Tydall had told her.

"Kellar the Great" appeared in Leadville on December 1, 1898, and wowed the crowd with his tricks. At the beginning of the performance, Kellar borrowed a ring from a member of the audience. He produced an ordinary bottle, pouring the best liquors into different glasses. Finally, he broke the bottle and out popped a cute, but dry, guinea pig, with the ring attached to its neck. Some of the audience did not think the trick was funny and insisted that the owner of the ring have it checked out to be sure that the magician had not conjured a different stone to replace the original.

On October 29, 1900, Alexander Herrmann and his wife appeared on stage to a sold-out audience. The first trick he played was to walk to center stage, take off his gloves and make them disappear. Next, he went into the audience and asked if he could borrow a gentleman's hat. When he had it, he pulled a rabbit out, threw it up in the air and shot at it; as soon as he did, the rabbit disappeared. They were not disappointed when he handed the gun to an audience member, asking, "Are you a good shot?" A bullet was fired at the magician's hand, and he caught it in midair.

Local lore says that Harry Houdini graced the stage of the opera house. Unfortunately, after exhaustive research, no documentation has been uncovered to prove that he was here, either under the ownership of Weston or the Elks Lodge.

All of Leadville turned out for a benefit hosted by the Eagles in February 1901 to pay for H.A.W. Tabor's funeral expenses, two years after his death. The *Herald Democrat* reported, "Leadville should be proud that Tabor's funeral was not paid for by the state." The house was packed, and extra seats had been added to the aisles. It was a variety of entertainment by Leadville's own: Leadville's Drum Corps played a collection of songs; Ethel Sandusky sang "My Heart To-Night in Texas"; a three-round sparring match took place between Paddy Purtell and Fatty Duell, well-known boxers; a

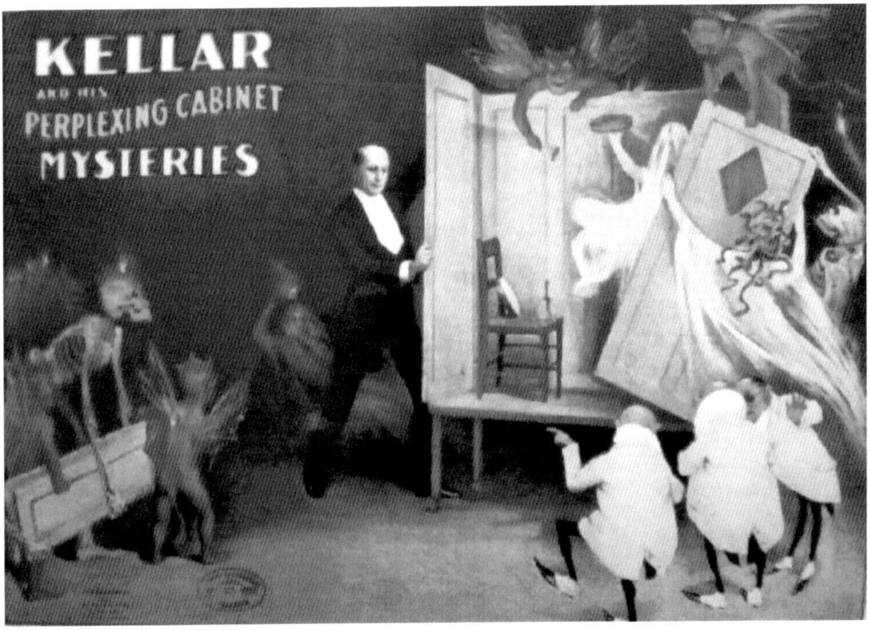

Poster of Kellar the Great.

wrestling match took place between "Dago" Mike and Fred Sherman; J.B. Dunn whistled "Blue and Gray"; Lottie Goldman showed the newest clog dance steps; and the Eagle Clarinets played "Le Absence et Le." Many in attendance were once friends with Tabor.

In 1894, Weston had taken out a loan for $10,000 at the Leadville Savings and Loan Bank against the opera house. By 1900, the loan was in default, and the opera house was sold at sheriff's sale. James Doyle of Cripple Creek purchased the property, and on April 18, 1901, he sold the property to Dr. Herron at auction.

That same month, the Benevolent and Protection Order of Elks Lodge 236 formed a building committee (Leadville Elks Building Association) with the purpose of finding a larger location for the lodge, and members appointed George Casey to be manager of all their properties. They sold $50,000 share of stock at $1 per share for the building fund. Other members of the committee included President Major A.V. Bohn and Vice-President Arthur Lumsden.

They looked at vacant lots and buildings to renovate but were having difficulty finding the right location. Dr. Herron tried to sell the property

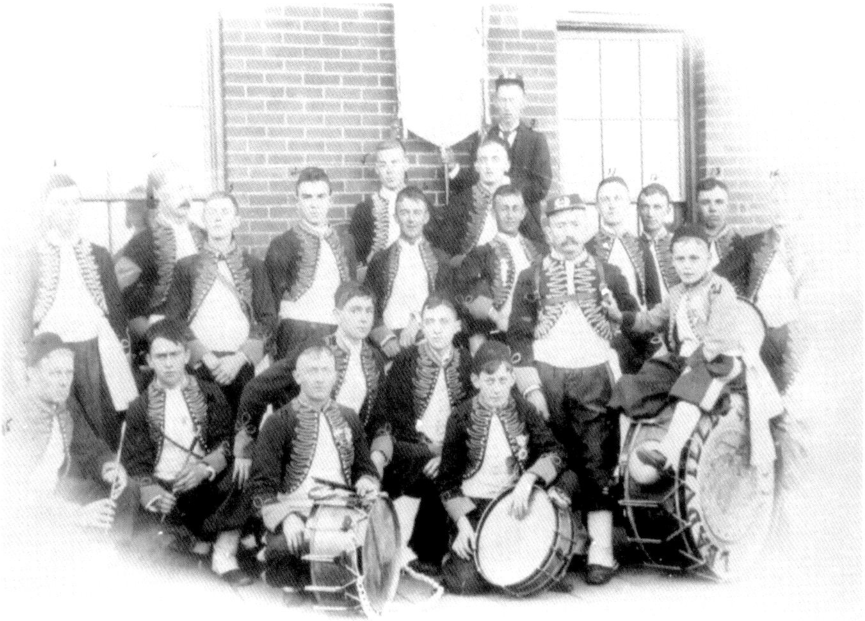

Leadville Drum Corps.

to the association; however, there was one small problem. Mrs. Weston and her sister were living upstairs and refused to leave. She demanded payment of $2,000, her perceived value of the building over and above the mortgage owed. Dr. Herron had no interest in managing theater performances and felt that the only way to remove Mrs. Weston was to close the theater. On May 1, 1901, the opera house became a dark stage for the first time in its history.

Unfortunately, George Casey, in anticipation of the Elks' purchase, had booked a full season of events. Casey was ordered to cancel all performances.

Some of the companies were due to arrive in less than a week and already had contracts. They could have sued Dr. Herron and forced him to allow them to play. Peter McCourt had also booked the Silver Circuit performances for the next year. All of them were canceled. Leadville citizens were very angry when they heard the news of the closing.

The Elks Opera House

The Elks Lodge finally purchased the building on August 11, 1901, for $12,500. The name was changed to the Elks Opera House. George Casey continued as manager, with Charles Mackenzie as treasurer. Casey contacted Peter McCourt and managed to get the opera house back on the Silver Circuit, and he even secured a few performances for the 1901–2 seasons.

The theater was cleaned and painted for the September 9 opening performance of *Molly G*, with the Joe Newman Company, and it opened to a packed house. Casey had his work cut out for him. While the theater was closed, the Lyceum Theater presented a new show every three days, and its stock company was very popular. The prices at the Lyceum were also cheaper, ranging from fifteen to thirty-five cents compared to the seventy-five cents the opera house charged.

On June 4, 1902, the opera house was closed for remodeling. A.G. Higgins, an architect from Pueblo, drew up plans for the entire building, including new clubrooms, a banquet room and a larger stage; the budget was not to exceed $25,000. Contracts were awarded to A.E. Schmidt ($17,221.00) for the interior; Mandy Brothers ($4,204.32) for steam heating, gas, plumbing and electrical; and to the Kansas City Scenic Company for new scenery and a drop curtain for the large stage. Many of these scenes still hang on the stage today.

The Elks planned to reopen with a first-class show and therefore set the opening date as December 11, with *Floradora*. This was the second season for the play, performed by a New York company. Several weeks before the reopening, Casey received a telegram from the Primrose and Dockstader Company, asking why the opera house wouldn't be ready on the tenth for their performance if it would be ready on the eleventh. During renovations, all engagements on the Silver Circuit were playing at the smaller, less popular Lyceum Theater.

Primrose and Dockstader was not a first-class company. The last time it played at the opera house, Primrose did not take the stage, and some of the actors were so drunk that they fell asleep on stage. Casey did not want this company for the grand unveiling, but Primrose and Dockstader's contract stated if the renovations were completed, it would perform at the opera house. It was indeed allowed to perform; however, the grand reopening was still the next night. The house was not full for Primrose and Dockstader, but there was a good-sized audience that enjoyed the show much more than its previous engagement.

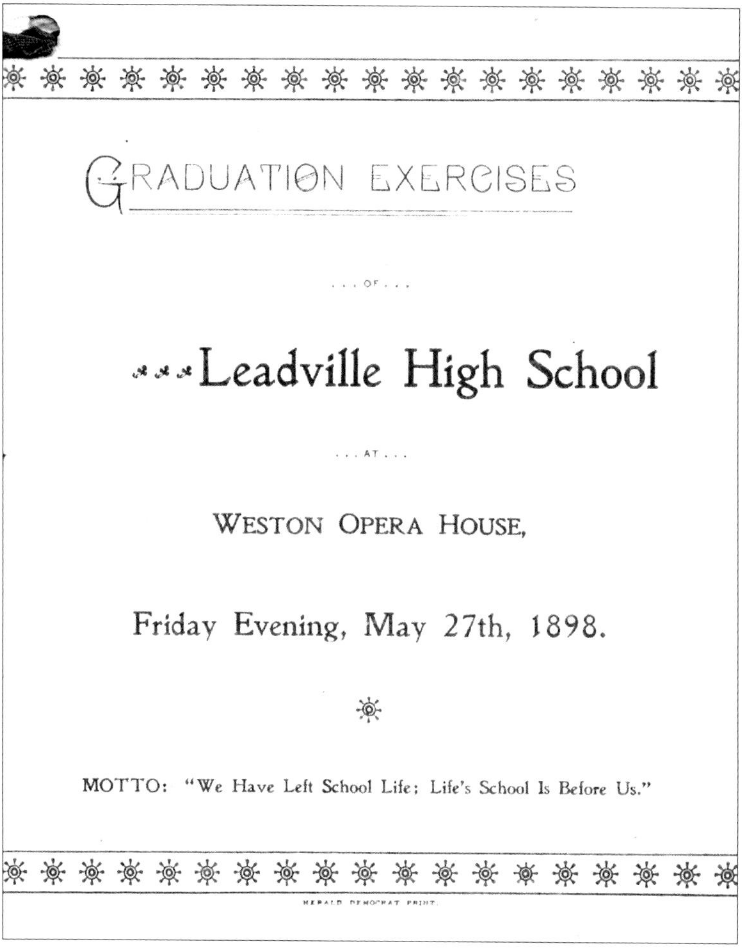

GRADUATION EXERCISES

. . . OF . . .

Leadville High School

. . . AT . . .

WESTON OPERA HOUSE,

Friday Evening, May 27th, 1898.

MOTTO: "We Have Left School Life; Life's School Is Before Us."

HERALD DEMOCRAT PRINT

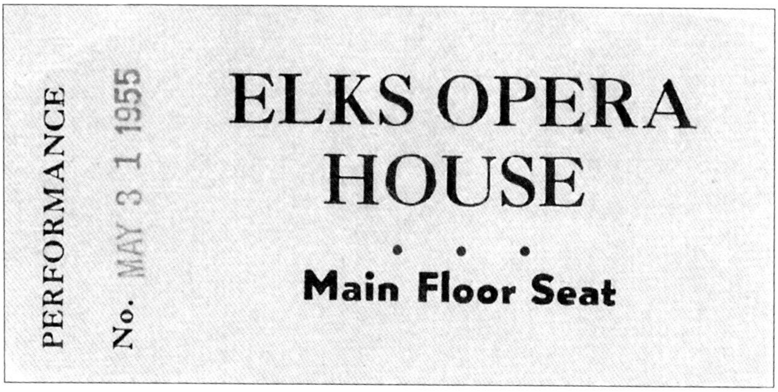

PERFORMANCE

No. MAY 3 1 1955

ELKS OPERA HOUSE

Main Floor Seat

ELKS' OPERA HOUSE

Friday, February 13, 1931

The Prospector Staff of Leadville High School

PRESENTS

"THE GHOST BIRD"

CAST OF CHARACTERS

ANDALUSIA ANDERSON, Mrs. Dore's hired girl .... STAFFIE DROBNICK
WILL BELMONT, Catherine's young brother .... HAROLD KELLY
TOBIAS TOLLIVER, An amateur detective .... JOHN KING
MRS. DORE, owner and mistress of the house .... DOROTHY O'BRIEN
CARL THOMAS, a young lawyer .... ROY SWANSON
CATHERINE BELMONT, a girl with an unwelcome suitor .... GERTRUDE McCARTY
PHILIP GRAHAM, who has rented the house .... WALTER MATSON
BRAD BUCKART, his friend and chief of detectives .... GEORGE CONKLIN
CELESTE, Catherine's maid .... ELVIRA CORTELLINI
BELLA WALKER, ANNIE BLOOM } Young girls of the neighborhood .... { EMILY SUE BOWDEN, JOSEPHINE PERKINS
JENKINS, a police detective .... HAROLD THOLEN
BUSINESS MANAGER .... JOSEPH McKEE

TIME: Early in the month of April.

PLACE: Mrs. Dore's old-fashioned farm house about forty five minutes from New York City

SYNOPSIS OF ACTS

ACT I—Living room of Mrs. Dore's home just before twilight on an evening in the month of April.
ACT II—Same as Act I. A few minutes later.
ACT III—Same as previous acts. About 8 p. m.
ACT IV—Same as previous acts. About 9 p. m.

AFTER THE PLAY FOLLOW THE CROWD!!!

WHERE?

WHERE DO U SUPPOSE?

Miller's Bakery & Confectionery

Previous page, this page and following page: Collection of opera house memorabilia. *Author's collection.*

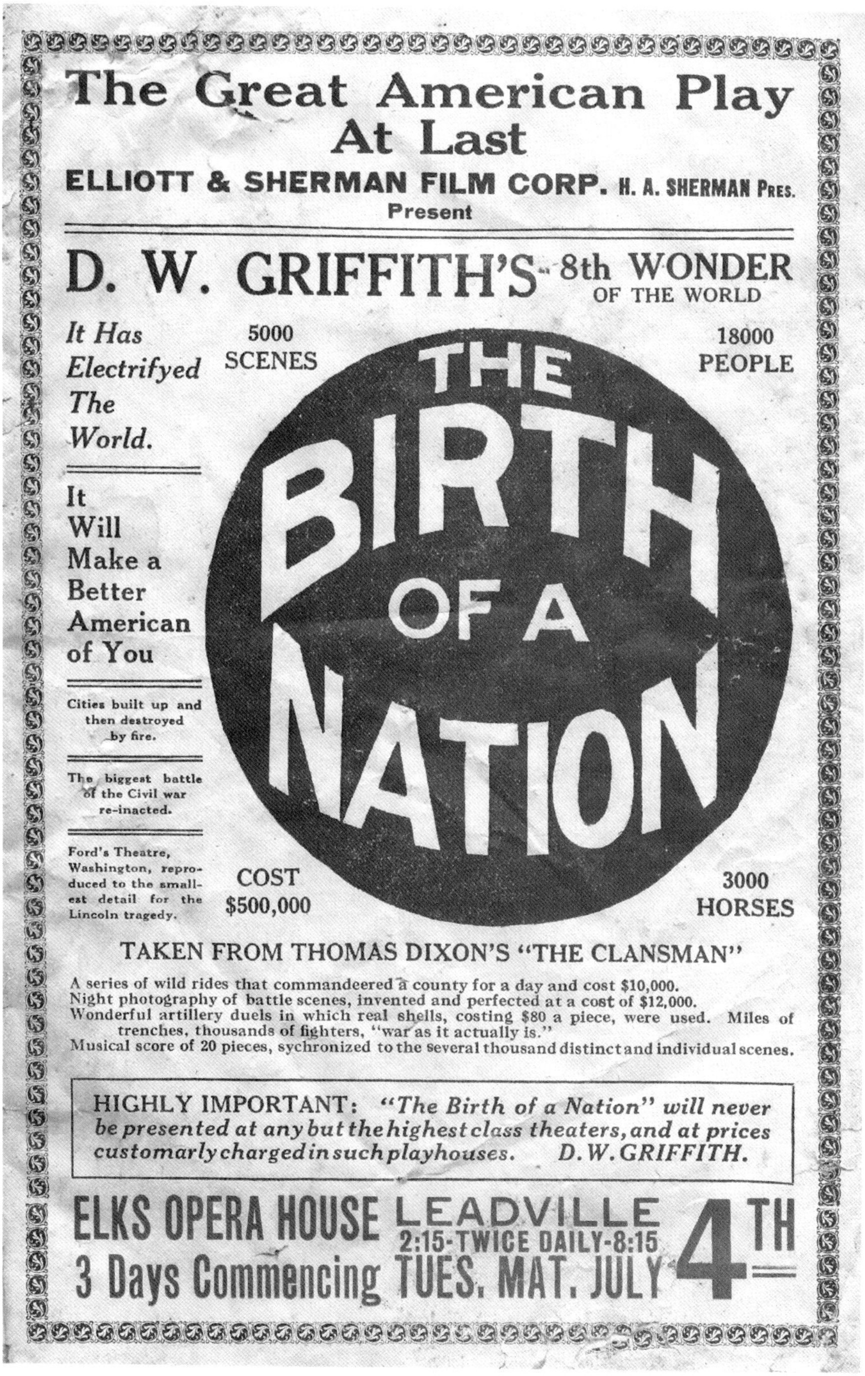
The Great American Play
At Last
ELLIOTT & SHERMAN FILM CORP. H. A. SHERMAN PRES.
Present
D. W. GRIFFITH'S 8th WONDER OF THE WORLD
It Has Electrifyed The World.
It Will Make a Better American of You
Cities built up and then destroyed by fire.
The biggest battle of the Civil war re-inacted.
Ford's Theatre, Washington, reproduced to the smallest detail for the Lincoln tragedy.
5000 SCENES
18000 PEOPLE
THE BIRTH OF A NATION
COST $500,000
3000 HORSES
TAKEN FROM THOMAS DIXON'S "THE CLANSMAN"
A series of wild rides that commandeered a county for a day and cost $10,000.
Night photography of battle scenes, invented and perfected at a cost of $12,000.
Wonderful artillery duels in which real shells, costing $80 a piece, were used. Miles of trenches, thousands of fighters, "war as it actually is."
Musical score of 20 pieces, sychronized to the several thousand distinct and individual scenes.
HIGHLY IMPORTANT: "The Birth of a Nation" will never be presented at any but the highest class theaters, and at prices customarly charged in such playhouses. D. W. GRIFFITH.
ELKS OPERA HOUSE LEADVILLE
2:15-TWICE DAILY-8:15
3 Days Commencing TUES. MAT. JULY 4TH

The next night, *Floradora* was enjoyed by a packed house. Everyone was anxious to see the renovations and the lodge rooms. The *Herald Democrat* reported that the "old barn-like theater was no longer recognizable; the new stage was a marvel."

On October 19, 1906, *Peggy from Paris* was scheduled, with leading man Arthur Deagon, known to be quite the joker. On the nineteenth, a man showed up and told a stagehand that Mr. Deagon was sick and wouldn't be performing. He fumbled about the stage, explaining that he would take Deagon's place. The stagehand sent for Casey, who was alarmed as the man continued to fumble about and thought about canceling the show. Finally, the man turned to Casey and introduced himself as Arthur Deagon. Luckily, Casey could take a joke. The show was a big hit, playing to a packed house.

Although the opera house was known for its legitimate theater, the management could not pass up the chance to make some extra money now and then. Ticket prices for boxing matches were twice what could be charged for the best traveling troupes, so the opera house also served as a sportsman's hall, hosting boxing and wrestling matches.

Well-known local boxer "Dago" Mike fought Hiach Smith of Nebraska, with Billy Irwin as referee, on February 18, 1920. In the first and second rounds, both men took turns punishing the other. The next few rounds went to Mike, who put Smith on the floor several times, but each time Smith got up before the count ended. In the sixteenth round, Mike pounded on Smith, landing him in the ropes and drawing blood.

When the bell rang for the seventeenth round, Smith entered the ring unsteady on his feet. Mike landed several blows to Smith's stomach and another to his jaw. Smith hit the ground, using the ropes to pull himself up. When Smith was on his feet, Mike rushed in, landing hard blows to Smith's jaw and knocking him out.

On March 22, 1903, an hour before the curtain was to rise on *Human Hearts*, George Casey realized that the troupe had not yet arrived. He went to the railroad station and was told that an accident had delayed the train by several days. Casey planned to shut the opera house, but audience members had already arrived. He and the staff put on an impromptu performance of *Closed Doors*. The skit, although funny, was not up to the normal standards the guests were expecting. Casey worked the announcement into the skit that the ticket price would be refunded; everyone got a good laugh and left happy.

Allen Curtis and his troupe played *Hooligan's Troubles* on April 20, 1905, but little did they know that their troubles had just begun. The next morning, as they were boarding the train to Denver, the owner of the

Manhattan Block arrived and demanded payment for the rooms they had occupied. The troupe assumed that Henry Astor, their manager, had paid for the rooms and the train tickets, as he had the money from the ticket sales. The troupe and their belongings were removed from the train, stranding them in Leadville. Astor had caught an earlier train, absconding with the money.

The Elks and Leadville were hosts to the Elks State Convention on June 14, 1907. Businesses decorated their windows in purple and hung welcome signs; many had an elk's head in their window. The welcome ceremonies were held in the grand ballroom with more than three hundred Elks officers and twenty members of the press in attendance.

Several special events were held for the Elks and their families, such as touring the Yak Tunnel Power Plant and the Silver Cord Mine. That night, a smoker was held in the clubrooms on the second floor. People told stories and sang. Later, they attended a private boxing match in the auditorium between "Kid" Texas of Leadville and "Young" Erlenborn of Denver; after ten rounds, the fight was called a draw. The next day, five thousand Elks and family members boarded a train for fun and games at Caledonian Park, west of Leadville, near the racetrack.

The opera house was renovated in 1914. The theater was repainted, restrooms were remodeled with new fixtures, dressing room furniture was reupholstered and the theater boxes were redone. When the opera house was reopened, it was greeted by a packed house. People were excited to see the changes.

One of the biggest changes was the production booth for moving picture shows. That year, the opera house had become a full-time movie theater, showing new films every three days. Although it continued to book some traveling shows, the emphasis switched toward movies. Critics pointed out that the opera house was greeted with a packed house for every traveling show.

On October 30, 1914, *The Shepherd of the Hills* was performed by Bess Dunlap and Van Morrell. The *Herald Democrat* reported, "Packed house last night indicates Leadville is starved for a taste of real drama. Hopefully, the management wakes up to the famine that has existed and will endeavor to relieve the condition."

Moving picture shows were booked at less cost. Some of the biggest films made their way to Leadville and were showed at the opera house, such as *Birth of a Nation* in February 1916. It was one of the most influential and controversial films of its time, one of Hollywood's first blockbusters. Set after

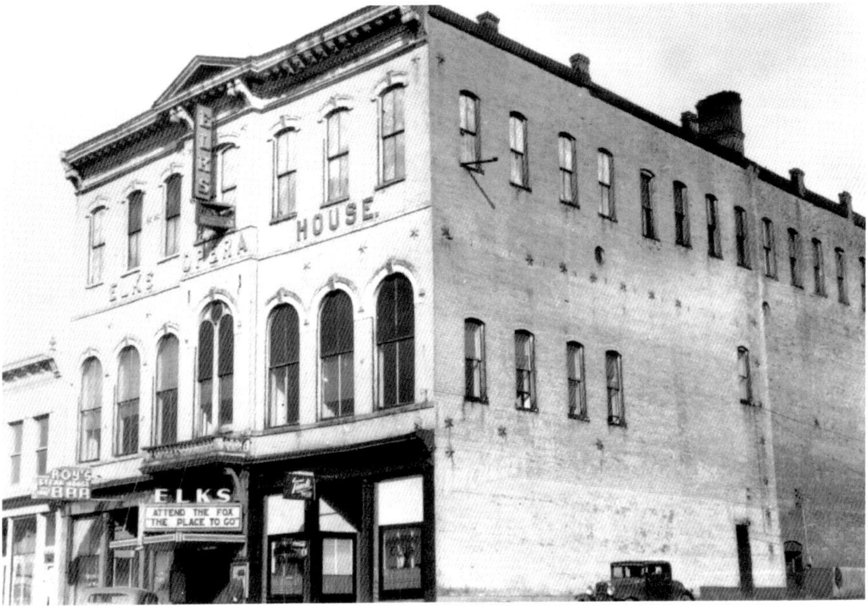

The Elks Opera House. *Author's collection.*

the Civil War, it was based on Thomas Dixon's book *The Clansman*. Everyone was excited to see if the actors, who had performed on the stage years earlier, were as good on the silver screen. Sadly, these silent films could not hold a candle to the real thing.

Another popular practice was to have vaudeville acts and moving picture shows at the same performance. The early moving picture shows tended to be more like historical documentation, such as shows about the war in Mexico or champion fight pictures. Later, they turned toward filming popular plays of the time.

J.E. Burgert of Universal Film Company came in the summer of 1915 to shoot a Leadville melodrama as a feature for Universal Animated Weekly. It was about a young couple in love; her father refuses to allow them to marry, so they plan to elope. When she gets caught in a fire, he rescues her, and they rush off to get married. The opera house was one of the locations chosen to showcase Leadville. St. George's Episcopal Church was another setting.

The feature that drew the most attention was the fire department, staging the rescue from a two-story home at 127 East Eighth Street. The fire truck rushed down the street, smoke pouring out the building, and the heroine was hanging out of the second-story window, crying "Help me!" Ladders were quickly put up, and the hero rushed up the ladder and grabbed his love, bringing her to safety. Elsie Cardinal, the heroine, said that she had trouble not laughing during the scene.

Several talented community members were featured in the film: Elsie Cardinal, Tom O'Mahoney, Gus Orven, Will Young, B.C. Gray and Fire Captain J.M. Tilloston. More than two thousand people turned out as extras, hoping that they would be in a crowd scene in the film. *The Romance of Leadville* premiered at the Elks Opera House on August 30, 1915, a few weeks after it was shot. Each showing was greeted by a packed house; they laughed as they caught sight of themselves or a friend in a scene.

A few weeks later, *The History of Leadville, 1850–1915* appeared at the opera house. This film, in three rolls and 1,500 feet long, showed pictures of Boughtown in 1850, later renamed Oro City, along with scenes in 1879 of the first courthouse, the post office and Chestnut Street. It had footage of the mining district showing the Tucson North Mine, the South Moyer Mine, the Yak Mill and Mining and the A.V. Smelter. There were several snapshots of Leadville citizens, some famous and some not so famous. It was once again a crowded house.

On November 24, 1915, Texas Ritchie, known as the "Gentleman Gorilla," came to play at the opera house. To promote ticket sales, Ritchie did a demonstration of his strength, pulling ten wagons full of girls down Harrison Avenue by his neck. He pulled them four blocks, from the Vendome Hotel to the opera house. The girls received free admission to the show.

Accompanying him was Marie Neville, who she swung six men around her neck at one time to show her strength. Ritchie topped this by swinging twelve men around his neck. Neville was considered "the perfect 36"—this was not about her age, as she was nineteen years old. She showed off the latest fashions and her "Garden of Eden" body and returned to the stage to bend pipe with her teeth.

Later, the "Gentleman Gorilla" took the stage and teetered twenty girls on his shoulders. Both Ritchie and Neville showed the audience that with the proper exercise, they could have the perfect figure. The next night, Ritchie challenged anyone with the same weight as Neville to box four rounds with her. It is unknown whether anyone took the offer. She did do a sparring match to show her skills in boxing.

In 1917, the opera house opened a new chapter in its history. It became a patriotic symbol of the war effort in Leadville. It donated space to the Red

Cross, which held many events to raise money. The Smokers Fund was also a frequent beneficiary of events at the opera house. The club bar donated a percentage of its proceeds.

Lectures pertaining to the war, from "How to Donate to the War" to "What It Was Like in the Trenches," were given to many packed houses. Also, the opera house was used as a recruiting place for young men to join the fight. As a result, many signed up to go overseas. Several were due to graduate from high school. On that same stage, their name was called, and they were issued a diploma even though they were not there to accept it.

Marion Kingsbury was hired in 1917 to run all local productions and benefit concerts. Marion, an opera singer with the Metropolitan Opera from 1904 to 1908, traveled abroad with the Conried Metropolitan Opera Company. She lived in Germany for a few years and joined the Opera Royal of Berlin before returning to Colorado at the outbreak of the war. She sang in four languages. When taking the stage in Leadville, men and women came to hear songs from their native land.

One of her most successful concerts was held on May 8, 1917, in front of a packed house. Marion wore a necklace that her father had made for her. Colonel Lemuel Kingsbury owned several mines in Breckenridge. As a child, she spent summers traveling with her father as he visited his mines. When she left for New York, he took a handful of gold nuggets from the Banner Mine and had a jeweler string them into a necklace. He had been offered $1,000 for it but refused, knowing that his daughter would treasure the gift. Marion received many compliments on the unusual gift.

Marion's main focus was to raise money to help the war effort. After this concert, she opened her own studio. Everyone was excited to sign up for lessons and train under such a talented singer. Her studio was located in the Chicago Block building on East Fifth Street. After a year, she moved to the Tabor Grand Hotel.

On September 12, 1938, a few men walking to work noticed flames coming out of the windows of the Club House Bar in the north-side storefront. Fireman were called and quickly managed to get the fire out. The owner of the bar came to assess the damage and noticed that several antique French paintings, valued over $3,000, had been destroyed. The fire was caused by a careless patron who left a cigarette burning. It fell on an overstuffed sofa, smoldering until it ignited the chair.

The fire became so intense that it blew out the front windows. It was lucky that the men noticed the fire, or the whole building would have been lost. The fire caused damage to the antique mahogany bar that had once been in the

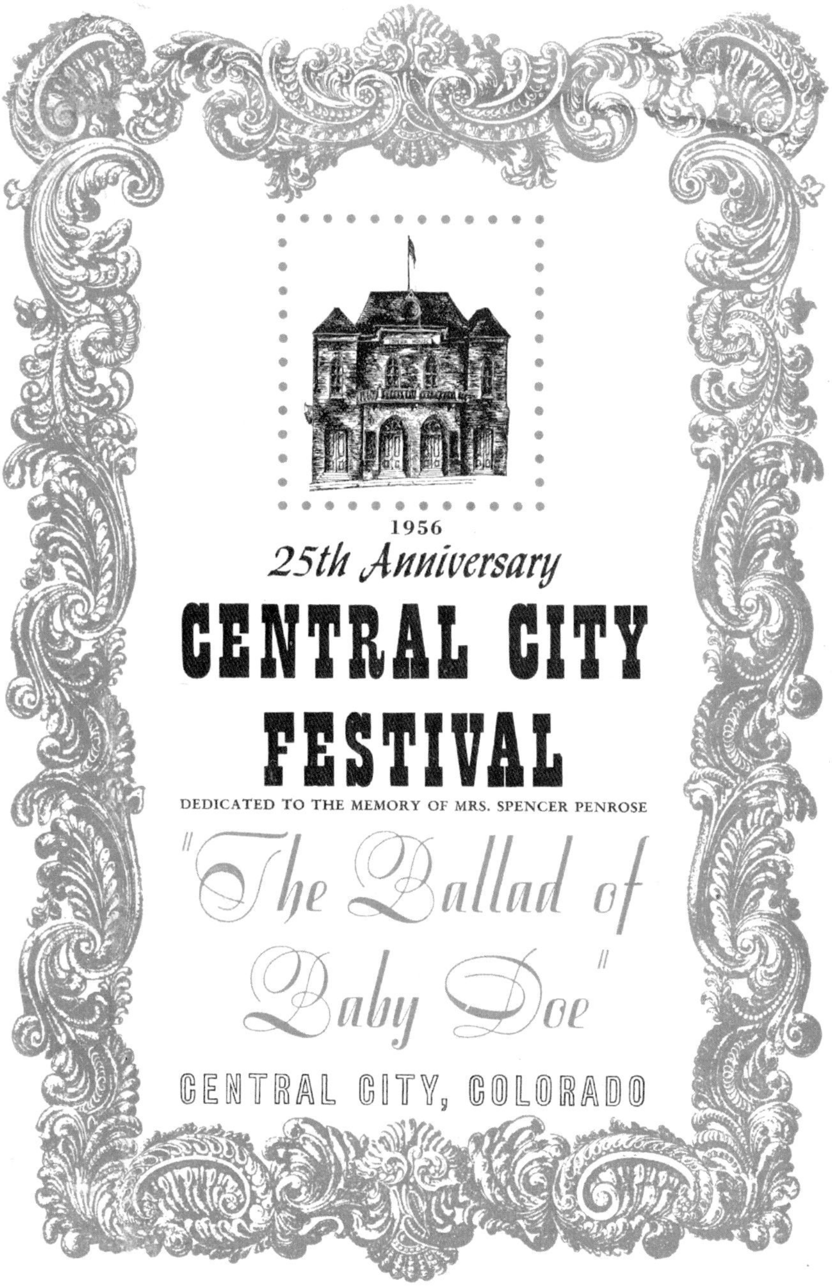

Program for *The Ballad of Baby Doe*. *Author's collection.*

Hub Saloon at 116 State Street. The fire was contained in the bar because of the eighteen-inch walls separating it from the theater.

It has long been thought that all the Andrew Make chairs remain in the opera house. Some are restored and on the floor of the theater, while others are stored in the attic. However, one is missing. It was given to Dr. Leroy Hafen of the Colorado Historical Society in November 1943 when he was traveling across the state gathering artifacts.

The Elks Lodge had considered selling the opera house for some time. It wished to build a new lodge that would be less costly to maintain. On December 22, 1954, members voted unanimously to sell the building to Florence Hollister. She promised the Elks that she would not demolish the building but rather would save it as a historical monument. The Elks retained the lease on the clubrooms for one year, until their new building was completed. Mrs. Hollister paid $20,000 for the building and contents. Florence Hollister and her daughter, Evelyn Furman, took possession on January 12, 1955, and reinstated the name, allowing the Tabor Opera House to live again.

The Ballad of Baby Doe, an operetta, brought the Tabor Opera House to the national spotlight again. The Central City Opera House Association commissioned Paul Green and Douglas Moore to write an opera about Baby Doe and Horace Tabor, specifying that it would be ready for the 1955 season and at least two hours long. Green and Moore would each receive $5,000. Caroline Bancroft was chosen as the advisor for the historical details—she did not receive any royalties. This would prove to be a fatal mistake, as Bancroft claimed that she owned the rights to the name "Baby Doe." She also believed that she had rights to the opera, claiming that any information about the Tabors belonged to her. The three of them could not reach an agreement, and each contacted an attorney to sue the others.

The Central City Opera House was running out of funds and joined with the Koussevitzky Foundation and Columbia University to finish the opera. Finally, they contracted with Douglas Moore and John Latouche. Shortly after this new partnership was formed, Latouche and Moore came to Leadville to visit the Tabor Opera House. Evelyn Furman had recently purchased the building, and it was still closed. The men went to her home and asked to be allowed in the opera house. It was a cold morning, but Mrs. Furman did not turn on the heat. She did allow the men to sit on the stage of the cold theater for a few hours, getting inspiration for the opera.

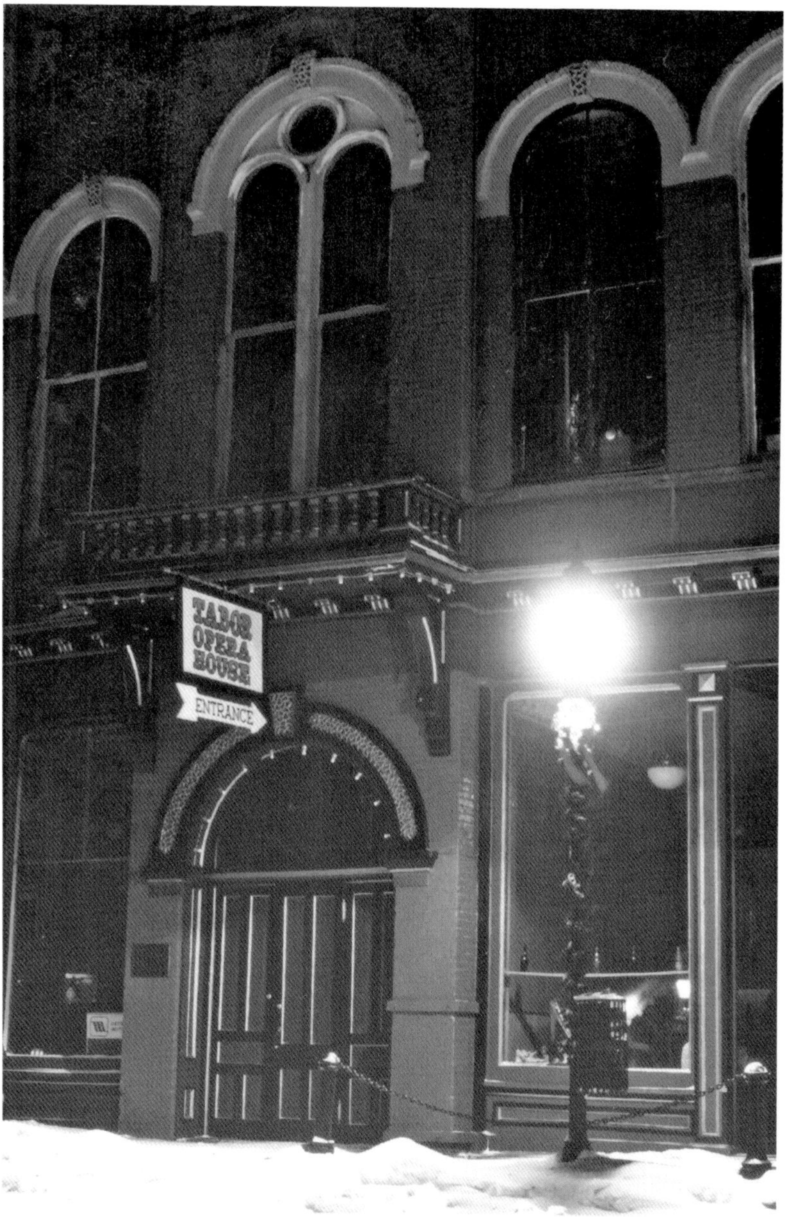

Tabor Opera House at night. *Author's collection.*

The opera did not finish on schedule. However, it premiered on July 7, 1956, and was a smashing success, bringing the Tabors and the opera house back to center stage. It is a very romantic version of the actual history. Some scenes are fiction, but it has kept the story from being forgotten.

Ownership has passed to Evelyn Furman's daughter, Sharon Bland, who continues the dream of her mother and grandmother. Restorations continue, through grants and fundraising efforts, to preserve this grand old lady for generations to come.

The Tabor Opera House, the last of Leadville's theaters, is open in the summer.

This house has been the forum for Leadville's brains and brawn,
In it we've honored those who lived and mourned for dear ones gone
In it we've voiced our hopes and fears—Our loves and our dislikes—have howled our deathless patriotism and even voted strikes,
It has echoed our endearments and we've watered it with tears
And its battered walls are eloquent with the sentiment of years

–Frank Vaughn 1905

Bibliography

Bishop, George W. *Charles H. Dow and the Dow Theory.* New York: Appleton-Century-Crofts, 1960.

Blair, Edward. *Leadville: Colorado's Magic City.* Boulder, CO: Pruett Books, 1980.

Busch, Stephen E. *Peter McCourt and the Silver Circuit.* Denver: Colorado State University, n.d. www.operahousepronto.com.

Carbonate Chronicle. January 1880–May 1921.

Colorado magazine, vol. 13, no. 3 (May 1936) and vol. 20, no. 6 (November 1943). History Colorado, the Colorado Historical Society, Denver, Colorado.

Daily Chronicle. January 1879.

Davis, Carlyle Channing. *Olden Times in Colorado.* Los Angeles, CA: Phillips Publishing Company, 1916.

Dearment, Robert. *Bat Masterson: The Man and the Legend.* Norman: University of Oklahoma Press, 1979.

Fields, Armond. *Eddie Foy: A Biography of the Early Popular Stage Comedian.* Jefferson, NC: McFarland & Company, 1999.

Gillan, Don. "A Brief History of American Theaters," 2007. Stage Beauty. www.stagebeauty.net.

Griswold, Don L., and Jean Harvey. *Carbonate Camp Called Leadville.* Denver, CO: University of Denver Press, 1951.

Harper, Ida Husted. *The Life and Work of Susan B. Anthony.* Vol. 1. Indianapolis, IN: Browne-Merrill Company, 1899.

Herald Democrat. August 1899–January 1923.

Hoyt, Edward Jonathan. *Buckskin Joe.* Lincoln: University of Nebraska Press, 1966.

Leadville Daily and Evening Chronicle. June 1880–June 1896.

Leadville Daily Herald. October 1881–October 1888.

Leadville Democrat. January 1881–June 1884.

Leadville Weekly Herald. November 1879–June 1881.

Mason, Stuart, ed. *Impressions of America.* Sunderland, England: Keystone Press, 1906.

Smith, Duane, with John Moriarty. *The Ballad of Baby Doe.* Denver: University Press of Colorado, 2002.

Turner, Tadd. "Wild Bill Hickok, Deadwood City: End of the Trail." Upublish.com, 2001.

Vivian, Imogene Holbrook. *A Biographical Sketch of the Life of Charles Algernon Sidney Vivian.* San Francisco, CA: Whitaker & Ray Company, 1903.

Wilde, Oscar. *Impressions of America.* Edited by Stuart Mason. Sunderland, England: Keystone Press, 1906.

INDEX

S

T

About the Author

Gretchen came to Leadville, Colorado, in 1999 and instantly knew that she was home. She spends much of her free time researching local theaters and early Leadville pioneers. Summertime finds her four-wheeling, geocaching and traipsing through the historic cemeteries.

Gretchen became passionate about Leadville's theaters while working as a docent at Leadville's famous Tabor Opera House. She never tired of hearing the many anecdotes about the early actors and actresses from Evelyn Furman, the opera house's owner. Her interest was piqued...and the rest is in the book.